WHO ART IN HEAVEN

PHILLIP H. HOOK

ZONDERVAN
PUBLISHING HOUSE OF THE ZONDERVAN CORPORATION
GRAND RAPIDS, MICHIGAN 49506

WHO ART IN HEAVEN

© 1979 by The Zondervan Corporation

Scripture quotations from *Revised Standard Version,* Harper Study Bible, copyright
  1952, 1946, and 1971 by Division of Christian Education of the National Council
  of the Churches of Christ in the United States of America.

Library of Congress Cataloging in Publication Data

Hook, Phillip, 1932-
    Who art in heaven.

      1.   God—Attributes.   II.   Title.
BT130.H6   231'.4   79-1365
ISBN 0-310-38191-6

Printed in the United States of America

*To those students
who have been my teachers*

Contents

Preface

A couple of years ago one of the men in a share group that I belong to asked us to evaluate what we'd change about our lives if we had only six months to live. This book is a result of that challenge. As I thought about it, I realized there were some things I wanted to say that I hoped would outlast my life.

What follows is what God has taught me through many books, many teaching sessions, many friends, and many students. It is the account of the beginning of what I intend to be a lifelong pursuit, however long that may be—the pursuit of knowing God.

Appreciation needs to be shown to many, many people because few of the thoughts here are really my own, but they have been learned from the people who thought I was teaching them. Special appreciation needs to be given to Pine Cove which allowed me to write as a part of my work and to Kathy Muntean who was both amanuensis and encourager.

PHILLIP HOOK

1

Wrong Gods

"Our Father, who art in heaven . . ." Nearly all young people in our part of the world learn to talk to God with these words. But, to whom are they talking? What is that heavenly Father like?

I'm a preacher's kid. My father happened to be a pastor of churches belonging to a very strict separatist group of churches. He was rigid in his own discipline, and often gone from home. My mother was a small and powerful person who could really pray. When Dad was gone and I was bad, Mom would pray and it seemed as if the heavens would "thunder."

These are my early recollections of an "earthly" father and mother who taught me what my heavenly Father was like. As a result, my early conceptions of God were of a rigid, legalistic despot who made everything go wrong unless I was good. I never went through the stages of atheism that so many young people go through. I believed in God, but I feared Him, dreaded what He would do to me if I made the slightest mistake, and was convinced He would make me do what I didn't want to do.

My life was governed by this concept of God. In fact, the quality of life we live will never be greater than the gods we have chosen to worship. What kind of a god is reflected in our lives? What thought or activity occupies most of our time?

1

What is the deepest motivation behind our actions? Answering these questions will give us clues to some of our gods. If we worship wealth, we will exhaust ourselves trying to earn lots of money. If we worship nature, we will expend much energy observing and studying it. By the same token, if our lives are spent following the examples Jesus taught, we will be exacting in our understanding of who God is. Within the range of possible gods, all of us have at least one.

In the New Testament, we see the scribes and Pharisees struggling with who Jesus is. They're caught with a preconceived idea of what God is like. This has grown out of their history, their culture, and the persuasions of their own lives. They have developed a concept of a god who is just like they are. He is separated from the world. (The word Pharisee means to separate.) This god avoids tax collectors, prostitutes, and other kinds of lost people.

At the same time, Jesus has a ministry that includes tax collectors, prostitutes, and sinners—people who are not normally accepted as part of the faith. Yet these people respond to Jesus in a remarkable and persistent way. They seem to sense in him someone who cares. One day when Jesus is ministering to the outcast group, the Pharisees raise the accusation found in Luke 15:2, "This man receives sinners and eats with them." The implication is that this Man must not be from God, or He wouldn't spend time with sinners; He would be like us. The Lord's answer to the accusation is a series of parables in which we often miss the purpose. We get preoccupied with the lost sheep and the prodigal son. We don't understand that the dominant description is of a shepherd who cares, a woman who searches, and a father who loves two sons. These parables present a unique description of what God is really like.

In the first parable, God appears as a shepherd who has lost a sheep. The shepherd cares about the one sheep so much that he leaves the other ninety and nine in the wilderness to go after the one which is lost. He doesn't scold the sheep for straying from the flock. Instead he picks it up and carries it with a heart joyful that the lost one is found. When he gets home, he calls all his friends and neighbors together and says, "Rejoice with me; for I have found my sheep which was lost!" (15:6). With the simplicity of the story of the shepherd, Jesus drives home an aspect of His character. He says, "Just so, I tell you, there will be more joy in heaven over one sinner who repents than over ninety-nine righteous persons who need no repentance" (15:7).

In this example, it hardly seems as if the remaining sheep are all lost and wandering, because all of them are together. In reality though, they are all in the wilderness and lost without the presence of the shepherd. If you look at the parable carefully, you will see that the one missing sheep ends up in the shepherd's arms. The rest end up straying in the desert. With the subtlety found in the parables, Jesus has taught the scribes and Pharisees two very important principles. Primarily, God is the kind of God who loves lost ones. Also, when people group together and agree on various issues without regard to any other influence, it may mean that they are the ones who are missing the fullness of a life such as the solitary sheep had that was carried by the shepherd.

Jesus uses a variation of this theme in teaching the parable of the lost coin. The woman's coins were not terribly valuable, but this was probably her dowry. The misplacing of only one coin caused her to be anxious. Notice the key phrase, does she "not light a lamp and sweep the house and seek diligently until she finds it?" (15:8). If the woman had applied common sense to the situation, she would have realized that the coin wouldn't move overnight. When daylight came the coin could easily be found. But the coin was of such great value to her that she searched her house diligently until she found it. Again, I think Jesus is saying to the Pharisees that God is the kind of God whose caring isn't dependent upon numerical value, but upon the understanding of the significance of what has been lost. The tax collectors and the sinners of society are of value to God not because of their monetary value, but because of their significance to a God who created them and loves them. Thus when the woman finds the coin, she has a party and says to her neighbors, "Rejoice with me, for I have found the coin which I had lost" (15:9).

The third story is usually, I think mistakenly, referred to as the parable of the prodigal son. Instead, it is the parable of the father, a man with two sons. There is a younger son, who was the prodigal, and an older one, who was possessive, self-righteous, and obnoxious. Being fed up with living in a home with a brother like that, the younger brother asked for his share of the property in advance and left the family. He feared that he would not get the inheritance after his father died and his older brother took over. Foolishly, he wasted all of his money and was forced to live with pigs and eat their food. It was then that the Jewish boy began to understand that his father loved him enough to let him go.

Deciding to return to his family, the boy prepared a speech for them. "Father, I have sinned against heaven and before you; I am no longer worthy to be called your son; treat me as one of your hired servants" (15:18–19).

When the son arrived, his father saw him and didn't wait for the speech. "But while he was yet at a distance, his father saw him and had compassion, and ran and embraced him and kissed him" (15:20). Not letting the boy finish his apology, the father put the ring on the son's finger, while the best robe and shoes were brought to him.

The older brother out laboring in the fields didn't understand his father's actions toward the younger, rebellious brother. Nor did he understand what his father was doing. When he heard signs of the party, he was at a loss to explain either the celebration or the return of his brother. A servant told him that his brother had come home and they had killed the fatted calf in his honor. But the brother "was angry and refused to go in. His father came out and entreated him, but he answered his father, 'Lo, these many years I have served you, and I never disobeyed your command; yet you never gave me a kid, that I might make merry with my friends. But when this son of *yours* came, who has devoured *your* living with harlots, you killed for him the fatted calf!'" (15:28–30).

We must understand that the older son never acknowledged that his brother had either a right to any of the estate, or a right to repentance. The father says to the older one, "Son, you are always with me, and all that is mine is yours" (15:31). The older son had lived possessing all of his inheritance. He never enjoyed it because he didn't understand the privilege of being a part of his family. He also missed that "It was fitting to make merry and be glad, for this your brother was dead, and is alive; he was lost, and is found" (15:32), for he never loved and appreciated his younger brother.

We see how the Pharisees and scribes were just like the older brother of the parable. They despised Jesus for His time with the publicans. They could not let God be loving, kind, or concerned about anyone's welfare but their own. Nor could they allow the lost and repentant ones to return. Our understanding of what God is like shapes the whole scenario of our lives. In our day, this country is captured by materialism. A man's life consists of what he possesses. Because of these misplaced values, we put importance upon where a man lives, the size of his home, the price of his car, and the kind of clubs to which he belongs. We use ownership of "things" as a mark of success. We do not ask if there's any joy to be found in having so much wealth. In fact, we become controlled by all of those possessions. We spend our waking hours preserving them, trying to make use of them, and trying to pay for them. Consequently, the materialism that is supposed to produce our joy becomes a wrong kind of a god that controls us.

There are many other groups in our country today that foster a wrong image of God. The hedonists worship the god of pleasure. Their constant search for happiness leads them along the path of the playboy or the playgirl, the path of drugs, drunkenness, sex, and all manner of destruction in God's design. As Romans 1 states, "They not only do them but approve those who practice them" (1:32). This group within our society worships at the altar of the god of leisure. The pleasures that they seek have no joy that will last. They're constantly caught in what Moses saw in Egypt, the "pleasures

5

of sin for a season." They hunger for bigger and better thrills. They find life burned out and empty before reaching middle age because their god is obsessed with having a good time or a pleasurable experience.

Other groups see God in different ways. Some Arminians within our evangelical theological circles have a god who is subject to the free will of man. He is a god who is incapable of acting because He is trapped by knowing what we're going to do and thus is limited by man's own will and similarly by man's choice. Therefore as God sits in the heavens, His hands tied by our will, we decide either to believe on Him or not to believe on Him. In the meantime, God waits patiently to see how we're going to turn out.

Some extreme Calvinists have a different idea of what God is like. Their emphasis on the sovereignty of God and the phrase, "before the foundation of the world," evidences a god who is captured by the plan that was made before the creation as we know it. Therefore, this god seems incapable of changing the world today because the elect are already chosen and there is no hope for the others. The result of this concept of God is that we sit on the sidelines waiting for that plan to be worked out.

Within neo-orthodox circles, there is a god who is so "wholly other" that He is not able to speak any clearer than a scratchy phonograph record. Vaguely He offers some direction, but He is not able to speak precisely in a manner knowledgeable of the Word of God. Therefore, because people have limited so greatly God's ability to speak, they must search the sunsets and the Scriptures for some experience or feeling to help them know Him.

The idea that our understanding of God shapes our understanding of the world is most clearly seen when we move to another culture. Most Oriental religions have a pantheistic concept of God, in which God resides in nature and in creation. Therefore their "heaven" or nirvana becomes the process of obliterating their own personhood and consciousness, and of becoming "one soul" with nature or creation. The goal is not to develop who they are in relationship to their Creator, but to obliterate that distinction as they seek to unite with the "mindless" creation.

This concept stands in sharp contrast to the revelation of Scripture, which says God is the Creator of all things and that He created man in His own image. Because of this, man is to worship the Creator and use the creation. Consequently, the part of the world influenced by Christianity eats beef, while parts of the Oriental world are overrun with sacred cows. The western world has developed science in order to use and accomplish something with creation, while the majority of the eastern world lives in squalor, unable to make much of creation work for them.

Contrasted to the worship of wrong gods, Psalm 19 gives a wonderful picture of the true God. I'm sure David developed this song out in the wilderness taking care of sheep when he was young. "The heavens are telling the glory of God; and the firmament proclaims his handiwork. Day to day pours forth speech, and night to night declares knowledge. There is no speech, nor are there words; their voice is not heard; yet their voice goes out through all the earth, and their words to the end of the world" (19:1–4).

In the twenty-four years that I've been involved in camping, many times we have started camp with this illustration as we sit out under the sky by a campfire, and look up to see what the heavens can tell us about God. Just from that setting we can determine that He is a God of order, a God of beauty, a God of immense size, and a God of enormous power who can talk to us constantly. The creative work that we see all around us is the product of His fingers. All of the intricacies observed in nature were carefully and creatively wrought by His hands. I am reminded of how my mother used to crochet. She would sit in the evenings working with her hands and making lace doilies for every chair and table in our home. The work of her fingers was evident throughout the house. Likewise, the work of God's fingers is noticeable throughout the universe.

There is more to God, though, than the work of His fingers. In the fifty-second chapter of Isaiah, we find another true manifestation of what God is like. He is speaking to Israel with regard to the joy that someday will be realized when they see God's redemption. "Break forth together into singing, you waste places of Jerusalem; for the Lord has comforted his people, he has redeemed Jerusalem. The Lord has bared his holy arm before the eyes of all the nations; and all the ends of the earth shall see the salvation of our God" (52:9–10). In creation we see the work of God's fingers, but in redeeming His people, the Lord has laid bare His holy arm which has great power behind it. Stop and think for a minute. To transform the life of a person, it takes a different kind of power than the effort it took to create the universe. This is the majesty of our God. While a revelation of Him is always around us, He really desires to make Himself and His power known to us in transforming our lives. The heavens are His fingerwork; His children are His real show of strength.

What kind of a God do we have? A God who doesn't care about lost ones? Who doesn't care about sinners? A God who is subject to the rules and the laws that we have developed? A God who is trapped by can't or won't? Or can we rightfully claim to know a God who lays bare His holy arm to redeem His people?

If we believe in the God of creation who created not only our surroundings but us as well, we bow before a supreme power who has ultimate love and control. Our world becomes a place for service, for caring, and for pleasure, because we are creatures in right relationship to a loving Creator.

STUDY QUESTIONS

While Jesus was here on earth, He often talked to people in parables. These were stories He used to explain in a simple way what He wanted to teach them. The different people who listened to Him or who were part of the parable can be identified in this way:

Tax collectors and sinners—these were people not accepted by the rest of the people in the community.

Pharisees and scribes—the men who lived a very strict

religious life according to the Old Testament laws. They were also the rich people in the community.

God or Christ—the One who comes to these people where they are living and is the answer to their needs.

1. In the parables found in Luke 15, about whom is Jesus talking?

2. In the Parable of the Good Shepherd who looks for the lost sheep (vv. 3–7), whom does the shepherd represent? The lost sheep? The ninety-nine?

3. In the Parable of the Lost Coin (vv. 8–10) whom does the woman represent? The lost coin?

4. In the Parable of the Father with the Two Sons (vv. 11–32), whom does the father represent? The older son? The younger son?

5. In each parable Jesus is teaching one thing that is most important. What is that in these parables?

2

False Images

No man lives without a God. The real question is who or what is his God, or gods. The pronouncement in the fifties and sixties that "God is dead" did nothing to God. Instead it simply attempted to assert that a certain God or kind of God was dead. I want to suggest that all of us have false images or concepts of God that we must cast aside. If you listen to people speak, and hear what they say, it is easy to see their image of God. For insight into this way of thinking, let's watch Jesus encounter false gods and display the story of the true God.

In John 8, Jesus had a great debate with the Jewish leaders around the statement, "I am the light of the world" (8:12). They denied this and accused him of being illegitimate (8:41, 48). After the final claim of deity by Jesus, "Before Abraham was, I am" (8:58), they took up stones to hurl at Him, and Jesus departed from their midst. As He left, He observed a blind man and the gods of several groups were revealed.

The God of the Disciples—Calamity Because of Sin

The disciples ask Jesus, "Rabbi, who sinned, this man or his parents, that he was born blind?" (9:2). And Jesus answered, "It was not that this man sinned, or his parents, but that the works of God might be made manifest in him" (9:3). In these

11

two simple statements the contrasting views of the disciples and Jesus come through clearly. The disciples' god makes children blind because of sin. This is often our approach to calamity. "Why did God make it happen?" Jesus doesn't answer the "why" question, but He penetrates deeper and says that there is a reason for the blindness. A problem or a calamity is an opportunity to see the power of God at work. You see, God has a purpose in that man being blind. He did not demand that it happen, but very surely, He allowed it to happen. The blindness is not a mistake. Rather it is a way to manifest the power of God in our lives.

If people have an automobile accident, is it because they were doing something wrong and God decided to punish them? Or if your life is going smoothly and is at present without conflict, is that an indication that God is rewarding you for good behavior? The God of creation doesn't necessarily inflict hardships, nor does He always offer rewards in order to bless His children. Instead, those incidents can be understood as a means, an opportunity, for God to fulfill His purposes.

An old ploy states: "How can a loving and powerful God have an evil world like this?" Or, "If God can't solve the problems I think up, He can't do anything." Many people think of God this way. God can't be all-powerful and loving and have an evil world like this. Therefore either He is not all-powerful, or He is not all-loving, or He is not God. In that case, there must not be a God, or else He is not a God who is worth wanting to know. Look at this diagram:

LOVING   POWERFUL   GOD
_____
EVIL WORLD

If we cross out loving and powerful, then we have to cross out God, according to this reasoning. What does that leave? All we have remaining in that case is the evil world.

~~LOVING~~ ~~POWERFUL~~ ~~GOD~~

EVIL WORLD

In addition, two rights are lost. The first is the right to call the world evil. By what standard is it evil if there is no God? Second, we have lost the right to hope. If there is no God then there can be no hope. There is only the world that exists. For better or for worse. But that is all.

At this point, we find the heart of the difference between Jesus' God and the god of the disciples. Jesus' God was one who changed calamity and despair for the blind man into sight and acceptance, while the disciples' god merely showed who he liked and disliked through his special treatments.

Jesus' God intervened in an evil world; the disciples' god was trapped by it.

The Bystanders—And Their God Who Can't and Won't

In the verses following, Jesus reminds the disciples of what He had said that had caused so much debate in the chapter before. He says, "As long as I am in the world, I am the light of the world" (9:5). Imagine, if you can, that you were there and watching what happened next. First of all, Jesus spit on the ground. And then He bent over and took that moisture and mixed it with dirt. When He had finished with that, He put it on the blind man's eyes. What happens inside your head as you watch the scene? Have you ever seen someone put dirt on a blind man's eyes? Have you ever seen anybody pull a trick like that on a blind person? At first observation, it looks like one of the dirtiest tricks anyone ever pulled off. But then Jesus said to him, "Go, wash in the pool of Siloam" (9:7). Now you can see that Jesus had a purpose in putting the dirt on the man's eyes. If Jesus had walked up to a blind man or to anyone and said to him, "Go wash in the pool," what likelihood is there that he would do it? But with dirt on his eyes, it guaranteed that he would wash.

In a way, the blind man sitting there with his cup is a pitiful sight. Even worse is somebody putting dirt on his eyes. But it is the design of God that sometimes things have to get worse before we come to the obedience which leads to healing. So the blind man goes to wash while the other people return to what they were doing, and Jesus continues on. But all of a sudden there's a noise. The blind man returns from the pool, and he can see. Then we witness one of those strange situations when seeing really isn't believing. The people have no category by which to understand a man who once was blind, and who now sees. The debate among the bystanders rages. "This is the man." "No, it's not the man." "Sure it is." "No, it isn't."

"I am the man" (9:9). Can you sense the frustration of the blind man, now healed, who knows he was in fact the one who was blind? At the same time the people around him are debating whether it is or not. The argument rages, you see, because the people have a god who can't, or who doesn't, do things like that. So they asked once again, "Then how were your eyes opened?" (9:10). He told them, "The man called Jesus made clay and anointed my eyes and he said to me 'Go to Siloam and wash'; so I went and washed, and received my sight" (9:11). Interestingly enough, the memory of dirt on his eyes is not something that he treasures. He doesn't say it was a dirty trick, nor does he say it was an awful thing. He only says that the dirt was the key to regaining his sight.

The people, wanting to see Jesus, said, "Where is he?" (9:12). But Jesus had slipped away and they didn't know where. Here you see the second false image of God: the god on whom we put limitations when we say he can't or he won't do certain things because they don't fit into our categories.

The God of the Pharisees—Bound by Man's Regulations

In Jesus' day the authorities were the religious leaders, and nobody was more religious than the Pharisees. Here we have a beautiful insight into what we can call the irony of God. Now the Pharisees who in chapter 8 took up stones to throw at Jesus have become the first witnesses of his miracle that revealed the truth of His claim; "I am the light of the world" (9:5).

There is one little problem though. It is the Sabbath day. When the man is brought to the Pharisees, he is asked how he received his sight. He says to them, "He put clay on my eyes, and I washed, and I see" (9:15). The Pharisees overlook that statement and say, "This man is not from God, for he does not keep the sabbath" (9:16). They are convinced that the miracle and the man are not from God, because it happened on the wrong day. However, there is nothing in the Old Testament that says you cannot heal a blind man on the Sabbath. Nothing defines that act as work. But the Pharisees, seeking to make God's Word plain and understandable, overemphasize the law about working on the Sabbath. Thus what Jesus had done in healing a blind man was against their interpretation of the Law.

In reality, their god was just like they were. He wouldn't heal on the Sabbath because he, too, is subject to the Law and their version of it. Therefore, they have made the same mistake that Israel made in the Old Testament in Psalm 50:21 when God accuses, "You thought that I was one like yourself." Because God had not judged them for their wrong, they assumed that He not only approved their wrong, but that He would have acted wrongly also. The Pharisees had picked up that same attitude, thinking that God would be no different than themselves. They couldn't heal the man on the Sabbath, and therefore, the man who did heal on their holy day must not be from God.

Strangely enough, they never deal with the miracle. They don't say that it is a miracle that this man was blind and now he can see. They simply say, "He can't be from God," which leaves only one other alternative if they accept this as a supernatural gift; he must be demonic. Fortunately, some of the other Pharisees recognized the miracle. They said, "How can a man who is a sinner do such signs?" (John 9:16). They called the healed man to account again. Instead of being judges of the case as the people intended, they turned judgment over to the man and asked, "What do you say about him, since he

15

has opened your eyes?" (9:17). Now the one who a few verses ago called him "the man Jesus," says, "He is a prophet" (9:17). But that testimony hasn't changed their reaction. The Jews did not really believe that he had been blind and had received his sight until they called his parents into consultation.

The God of the Parents—The Peer Group

Once again, imagine that you are there. As this debate about the miracle and the person of Jesus continues, somebody goes to get the parents and brings them to the crowd. I would imagine during the trip there was a time of telling the parents what had happened, so that when they arrive, they see the dissension. The Pharisees are on one side saying, "No." The healed man is on the other side saying, "I've been healed." The people want to see how his parents will respond to this miracle. They are asked, "Is this your son, who you say was born blind?" (9:19). An astounding answer comes from his parents. "We know that this is our son, and that he was born blind; but how he now sees we do not know, nor do we know who opened his eyes. Ask him; he is of age, he will speak for himself" (9:20-21). Such was their response, since they knew that if people confessed this man to be the Christ, they would be put out of the synagogue.

During the time that they were coming to witness this scene, surely the parents had been informed about the healing and resulting disbelief of the Pharisees. Therefore, they denied that they believed the miracle because their god is the god of the group, the god of peer pressure. In reality, their god was far away and their only fear was the god of whoever is near at hand.

I remember an instance as a dean of students when I called in a student in regard to a medical report he had turned in. For some reason, after he left, I questioned the validity of his excuse of illness, so I called the doctor. In talking to his secretary, I discovered that the doctor had been on a hunting trip for two weeks. It was impossible for him to have seen the student. So I called the student back and discovered that there had been a pattern of lying in his life. As I confronted him with that pattern he said, "You know, Dr. Hook, I am more afraid of you than I am of God, and that's why I lied to you." Just so, these parents of a blind child found their god in the pressure of the peer group, rather than in the God who really touches and heals people.

The God of the Blind Man—Listens Only to Good People

Following this, the leadership tries again to convince the blind man that Jesus is not from God. They say to him, "Give God the praise; we know that this man is a sinner" (9:24). Once again, this is like so many people in our world who have a general belief in God, but who will not come face to face with the evidence of God. They love to say, "God bless you," and then they do not connect anything in this world with what God is really doing.

The man in his logic responds to their request. "Why this is a marvel! You do not know where he comes from, and yet he opened my eyes. We know that God does not listen to sinners, but if any one is a worshiper of God and does his will, God listens to him. Never since the world began has it been heard that any one opened the eyes of a man born blind. If this man were not from God, he could do nothing" (9:30–33).

The fascinating thing is that while his logic overwhelms his audience, within it there is another view of God that is faulty. "We know that God does not listen to sinners" (9:31). This blind man, who spent all of his life as an outcast waving a cup and asking for alms, really believes deep down inside that God only hears the nice people, the good people, the perfect people. While the logic on that premise is inescapable and the audience with which he is debating accepts it, he, too, appears to have a faulty view of God. But they said, " 'You were born in utter sin, and would you teach us?' And they cast him out" (9:34).

Next, take a look at Jesus' beautiful answer to what God is like. "Jesus heard that they had cast him out, and having found him he said, 'Do you believe in the Son of man?' " (9:35). The man had been cast out, and in a way, he was right where he had started the day—as a blind man alienated from society, waving his cup and asking for alms. Now he has finished his day, an outcast from society but no longer waving his cup, because he had no reason to beg. We can realize a difference, because now he can see. Now he has someone who cares about him, because Jesus, rather than casting him out, went looking for him. When He found him, Jesus asked, "Do you believe in the Son of man?" And the man answered, "And who is he, sir, that I may believe in him?" Jesus said, "You have seen him, and it is he who speaks to you" (9:35–37).

Do you see the sequence of those questions? Jesus asks, "Is there faith?" The man's faith is such that he says, "You say it, and I believe it." To that kind of man the Lord God responds perfectly with a complete answer. "It is He who speaks to you. You have seen him." Seeing—the sense he couldn't use at the beginning of the chapter—now becomes a possibility with the eyes of understanding. So he can say, " 'Lord, I believe,' and he worshiped him" (9:38).

You see, God shows the blind man that he's more than just a God who listens to nice people, to good people, to perfect people. He also hears blind people, people who have been cast out, people who are alienated from their society. Jesus searched for him—an outcast from humanity. Like the shepherd in search of the one lost sheep, the God of the Savior cared about this man enough not only to find him, but also to reveal Himself to him, because "Without faith it is impossible to please him. For whoever would draw near to God must believe that he exists and that he rewards those who seek him" (Heb. 11:6). We can begin to understand the calamity of anyone who considers God to be any less than He really is.

STUDY QUESTIONS

A blind man, who had never been able to see, was healed by Jesus and, for the first time, he could see. Because it was so unusual and had never happened before, it caused people to think about God.

False Images

1. When Jesus and His disciples first saw the blind man, what did the disciples think? What does this tell you about their idea of God?

2. What did the Pharisees think about the miracle? Did they really believe the blind man was healed? What did they think God is like?

3. If someone close to you, such as your brother, had been born blind, how would you feel if he came home running with joy because he had suddenly regained his sight? What were the blind man's parents like? How did they think of God? Did they believe their son was healed by God?

4. What did the blind man think God was like? Would you agree with him?

5. What can you learn about God through the account of Jesus healing the blind man?

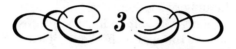

God Is Spirit

To understand God as spirit is perhaps the most fundamental concept of God that we can have. The circumstances are fascinating under which God chose to reveal one of the most significant statements about His spirit that is made anywhere in Scripture. Let's take a look at John 4 and notice how God chose a woman of not particularly good reputation, out in the middle of nowhere, during the heat of the day, and revealed His deity to her in a very special way.

We would have acknowledged God's presence differently because our knowledge of technology and advertising dictates having the television cameras and the important thinkers and philosophers present. But God's ways are not our ways. For some reason or another, He made this tremendous theological statement about Himself as spirit to a woman, a Samaritan of bad reputation, out in the middle of the desert.

What Is Jesus Like?

Think about what God is like in regard to that woman in Samaria. Our society today is trying to work through the role of women, and is having a certain amount of problem in the process. Sometimes the church has had a bit of trouble that way, too. Many women feel they are poorly qualified for service in the church. They feel they're not able to do anything because God doesn't think they are significant. Stop and think about what kind of a God it is who takes a statement as profound as this one and, without trumpets and fanfares and fire and lightning and skywriters, says it very quietly to a woman. It becomes a life changing experience for her and for her community.

An understanding of the long time dissension between the Jews and Samaritans will help to illustrate Jesus' conversation with the woman at the well. The Samaritans probably grew out of the time that most of the Jews were in captivity. Some Jews were left behind in Israel and intermarried with the surrounding nations. These half-Jews retained some of their heritage, but their temple and city had been destroyed by the conqueror and they were just living in the area. When God brought part of his nation back with Ezra and Nehemiah, these were probably the people who offered to help. But Nehemiah had to tell them they couldn't participate in rebuilding the temple because they had intermarried with the other nations. They weren't qualified to be a part of it. At that time they became archenemies of the rebuilding of the city and of the temple.

Ultimately, they went a few miles to the north and built their own temple with their own copy of the Five Books of Moses, also known as the Samaritan Pentateuch. Samaritan worship was an imitation of the Jewish worship. For this reason there was a tremendous amount of anger and hostility between the two groups. So much so that a Jew going from Jerusalem to Galilee wouldn't even walk through Samaria, although it was the shorter route. He went down across the Jordan River at Jericho and up on the east side of the Jordan River, then back across up by the lake of Galilee. This was so he wouldn't have to defile himself by walking through Samaria.

With this in mind, try to imagine what it was like for Jesus, a Jew, to strike up a conversation with a Samaritan woman. Jesus had been in the southern part of the country for a short while and then he started back up into Galilee. Attention is focused on him now. "When the Lord knew that the Pharisees had heard that Jesus was making and baptizing more disciples than John, he left Judea and departed again to Galilee. He had to pass through Samaria" (John 4:1–4). He took the shorter route not because it was short, but because he had important business to do. "So he came to a city called Sychar, near the field that Jacob gave to his son Joseph. Jacob's well was there, and so Jesus, wearied as he was with his journey, sat down beside the well. It was about the sixth hour" (4:5–6).

"There came a woman of Samaria to draw water. Jesus said to her, 'Give me a drink' " (4:7). The woman would not ordinarily be called a lady, because she had had five husbands and the man she had slept with the night before wasn't one of them. Sometimes it is said that she was out drawing water in the heat of the day because she was unacceptable to the other women in town. Another theory is that she had just gotten up to begin her day, because her hours were different from the other women.

For a little while, put yourself in her place. You are a Samaritan. You are a lady of ill repute who has just gotten up and gone out to draw water in the heat of the day. You come to the well and a Jewish man asks for a drink. We must be able to visualize the encounter in order to understand it. Try to work your way through the conversation that Jesus has with the woman. Remember that Jesus had to go through Samaria, perhaps to satisfy a compulsion to minister to all people. Also keep in mind that He did not withdraw when the woman came to the well as a Jew might have done. When she came, He talked to her as a person, because He really cared about her.

Encounter with a Jew

"Jesus said to her, 'Give me a drink.' For his disciples had gone into the city to buy food. The Samaritan woman said to him, 'How is it that you, a Jew, ask a drink of me, a woman of Samaria?' For Jews have no dealings with Samaritans" (4:7–9). What do you suppose is going through her mind? With her limited understanding of who He is, she probably considers Him a potential customer for her services. But what has Jesus done when He asks for a drink? He has accepted her to a certain extent, opened a way of communication, and asked a favor of her. Isn't it strange that He is going to place Himself in her debt?

Look closely now at her reaction. "How is it that you, a Jew, ask a drink of me, a woman of Samaria?" (4:9). What tone of voice do you think she used? Sarcastic perhaps? The moment He says He will take her cup and drink of it, he sacrifices His Jewish heritage. A good kosher Jew doesn't risk eating or drinking out of non-Jewish utensils. What could Jesus be trying to say? The woman misunderstands Him completely, but Jesus says to her, "If you knew the gift of God, and who it is that is saying to you, 'Give me a drink,' you would have asked him, and he would have given you living water" (4:10).

What is going through your head right now? If, as the Samaritan woman, you only knew the gift of God and who it is that is talking to you, would that change your reaction? Who does that sound like in our society? Muhammad Ali? Other outspoken leaders, perhaps? From a human point of view, it has to be one of the strangest, most egotistical statements ever uttered. Remember that we know who He is, and at this point, the woman did not.

Continuing to miss Jesus' intended meaning, she says, "Sir, you have nothing to draw with, and the well is deep; where do you get that living water? Are you greater than our father Jacob, who gave us the well, and drank from it himself, and his sons, and his cattle?" (4:11–12). What tone of voice do you think she's using now? Probably it hasn't changed much from her previous somewhat cynical statements. She's asking who He thinks He is to ask such a question of her. This is a prime illustration of how often people miss what God is saying to them because they interpret it in the light of their own experience.

In John 3, Jesus says to Nicodemus that he must be born again, and what does Nicodemus say? "How can a man be born when he is old? Can he enter a second time into his mother's womb and be born?" (3:4). This woman is no different. Another example of this is found in John 5, when Jesus comes to the man at the pool at Bethesda and asks him if he wants to be healed. And what does the man say? "I have no man to put me into the pool when the water is troubled" (5:7). He could have accepted Jesus' offer. You see though, he doesn't understand what is happening, so he misses the chance to know Christ. In repeated instances, the people miss much of His meaning.

I recall a telephone conversation with someone several years ago. We were praying for a family in which the father had just accepted Christ and the mother had not. I had asked another friend of mine in the area to visit her. So I called the now Christian husband to tell him what I had done. He said to me, "You know, about three or four years ago, she wrote us a long letter asking us about trusting in the Lord. We thought it was sort of silly."

That is the way we often are; we remain oblivious to what God is doing. Do you see that this is exactly what is happening to the woman at the well? She cannot understand how she can get living water from a well which contains only regular drinking water. Graciously Jesus responds to her, "Every one who drinks of this water will thirst again, but whoever drinks of the water that I shall give him will become in him a spring of water welling up to eternal life" (4:13–14). What do you suppose she is thinking? Why has this woman remained at the well this long? Why didn't she return to her house? Obviously, her curiosity is aroused and she wants to find out who this Man really is.

Encounter with a Prophet

Even though she still misunderstands Jesus' offer, she says, "Sir, give me this water, that I may not thirst, nor come here to draw" (4:15). What does she understand of Jesus? At the very most, she thinks she has found someone like the prophet who provided food during the famine long ago. But look at what the Lord has accomplished in the woman's life. He has her attention; He has appealed to her needs; He has shown an interest in her. This is one of the strangest approaches she's ever faced as a woman of the street.

Dramatically, the Lord changes the entire nature of the conversation. She didn't expect Him to say, "Go, call your husband, and come here" (4:16). It is hard to know what she was thinking when He said this to her. But her statement, "I have no husband" (4:17) would normally have left the conversation open for whatever proposition he might offer. Jesus responds, "You are right in saying, 'I have no husband'; for you have had five husbands, and he whom you now have is not your husband; this you said truly" (4:17–18). Now the conversation has taken a completely different turn. In a sense, they were only sparring about the water. Jesus was serious, and so was she, but they were serious about different things. Now at least they are getting down to a subject that both of them understand.

She says to Jesus, "Sir, I perceive that you are a prophet" (4:19). What do you think she is going to do? If Jesus is indeed a prophet, what is the next thing? He needs to be put to a test to see if He is real. The procedure of the day was to ask some suitable theological question. This was often done to Jesus. Therefore, she responds in this pattern, first thinking Him to be a prophet, and then asking Him a question. "Our fathers worshiped on this mountain; and you say that in Jerusalem is the place where men ought to worship" (4:20). There is the test, and Jesus answers, "Woman, believe me, the hour is coming when neither on this mountain nor in Jerusalem will you worship the Father. You worship what you do not know." (4:21–22). Here is the first part of His answer. He tells her that the Samaritan worship is false because it is without a God. The only true worship is God-given.

Encounter with the Christ

The second part of the answer is, "We worship what we know, for salvation is from the Jews" (4:22). What is He telling her now? That the true God has revealed Himself in Israel. If she is going to have a Savior, who must it be? Inescapably, we know that it must be Jesus, a Jew. "But the hour is coming, and now is, when the true worshipers will worship the Father in spirit and truth, for such the Father seeks to worship him" (4:23). Going one step further, we recognize that worship will change in its nature. Up until now their formal worship has been in a temple, through a ritual of sacrifices. Now, however, it is going to change, for he says, "God is spirit, and those who worship him must worship in spirit and truth" (4:24).

Still, the woman was missing Jesus completely. She was thinking of water which has a chemical composition of hydrogen and oxygen, only she wanted an ever-flowing supply of it. On the other hand, Jesus was talking about water in another realm—the realm of the Holy Spirit.

For a definition of God as spirit, let's look at Second Corinthians 4. "But we have this treasure in earthen vessels, to show that the transcendent power belongs to God and not to us" (4:7). You see, the ministry is God working, not man. "We are afflicted in every way, but not crushed; perplexed, but not driven to despair; persecuted, but not forsaken; struck down, but not destroyed" (4:8–9). Paul could handle the problems of life because he saw the reality of what the ministry was, and that's the glory of God at work. "So we do not lose heart. Though our outer nature is wasting away, our inner nature is being renewed every day. For this slight momentary affliction is preparing for us an eternal weight of glory beyond all comparison, because we look not to the things that are seen but to the things that are unseen; for the things that are seen are transient, but the things that are unseen are eternal" (4:16–18). The realm of reality is not the material time-space realm of this world. The "real reality" is the realm of God—Spirit.

What has Paul just said? The problems of this world are not ultimate. They are necessary to the nature of this life. And we have this treasure in earthen vessels. The emphasis is not on the earthen vessels; in fact, that's what makes it obvious that God is at work. The significant thing is what we have in relationship to God. Therefore, we're to be honest in our proclamation of the Gospel. In light of that, we don't worry about the persecution, and the deteriorating body that we all live in

27

isn't important. All of these things are going to pass. Everything in the world is going to pass. It all gets old and it all deteriorates. This world is real, but it is real only by creation. Pain, affliction, and the persecution are real. But God created this world and put us in it. The reality that is eternal is not this world, it is the relationship with the Creator Himself. The problems prepare us for the glory that will be ours with Him in the eternal world.

Another parallel passage may help us understand this. In proclaiming the message of the Sermon on the Mount, Jesus reached the high point when He said, "But seek first his kingdom and his righteousness, and all these things shall be yours as well" (Matt. 6:33). Jesus is retaining this same perspective of reality. When our goal is in the proper realm, then our understanding of the realm of the material will be in proper perspective, too. This is the heart of Paul's understanding of the ministry. "Though our outer nature is wasting away, our inner nature is being renewed every day" (2 Cor. 4:16).

Something in man that corresponds to God is real and not physical. I can't tell you what a spirit is, nor can I offer you a handful of spirits so you can touch them and understand what they are. Spirit is the realm of God—the realm of the eternal. It is also a part of what is to be found in man, something that isn't tied to the material. This truth is the foundation of our relationship with God.

When God created us in His image, He didn't give us physical features similar to His, for God's realm is not that of ears and noses and complexions. But God did place within us something that makes us comparable with Him. If we were to die today, our bodies would remain, but that in us which is spiritual would be gone. This is the realm of God—God is spirit. And He says we who would know Him and worship Him must do it in that perspective. At this point, prayer and praise become understandable in the realm of the spiritual. We can know Him. We can sense His presence and we can talk to Him.

When I was on the spiritual life committee at a Christian

college, one of our responsibilities was planning chapels. Four days a week we arranged them, and one day a week the students did. One day we went into a student service. All the furniture was gone from the platform, and there was only one great big black cross, which the students had hung over it. They announced that we were going to have a liturgical service. It was a beautiful worship experience, using all the elements involved in an extensive liturgy. Several days after this service a memo came down from the administration, "Take down the black cross." It was dutifully removed from the chapel and stored somewhere on campus. That weekend, the students found it and put it back in the chapel. Once again a memo came from the administration to remove it, and this time it was destroyed. But once again, the following weekend, the students made a new cross and put it up. Thus it became the responsibility of the spiritual life committee to settle the issue between the students and the administration.

We called the students in, and they said they couldn't worship without the cross. The stage was too barren and the lack of religious symbols hindered worship. We called in the administration and they said, "We are a college of the reformation. The center of our worship is the open Word of God. We don't need symbols or other focal points of worship." Both sides were really missing the heart of the issue. Worship is an awareness of God's presence, and there are many circumstances and occasions when that worship takes place. God's presence is in the realm of spirit, to which we can tune in any time. I could worship in chapel or in class or walking across campus or in my office or wherever I was because God is spirit and therefore not confined to a particular setting.

However, every spiritual experience isn't necessarily a worship experience of God. So Jesus builds into His statement a careful protector. We must worship in spirit and in truth. A young girl came into my office one day and proclaimed to me that God had told her she should marry a non-Chrisitian. This left me with conflicting "truths," because God's Word has made clear that we shouldn't be "yoked to unbelievers." Yet, she told me that her worship experience with God had taught her contrarily to God's Word. This cannot be. Therefore, God has given us a very clear guideline and corrective for our worship. Whenever our worship doesn't accord with what He has said, then it is probable that we've confused the spirit that we're worshiping. We may simply be communicating with ourselves or else with Satan.

The breadth and beauty of true worship is portrayed for us in the Psalms. The desecrating horror of false worship is ever present in the cults, which usually have a fragment of truth making them plausible. But they deny the "truth," and this makes them wrong.

To know God as spirit gives us the frame of reference to understand that which we worship and also the material world around us. Christianity doesn't deny the reality of the world, but it asserts that its reality is secondary. It demands that, first of all, we must relate ourselves to the realm of God and to His kingdom. Then we have a proper view of God and His world.

I believe that the Lord was teaching this to His disciples specifically when He sent them forth two by two and said for them "to take nothing for their journeys except a staff; no bread, no bag, no money in their belts; but to wear sandals and not put on two tunics" (Mark 6:8–19). They were to place first in their emphasis the ministry that God had given them. Then all other things would fit together. Sometimes the crushing burden of American Christianity is that we've confused the abundance of things with the reality of God's favor, just as Israel did. In so doing we have created a whole new realm of worship. So worried are we about perpetuating all the things that we miss the joy of His presence.

Recently, I sat in the midst of some Eastern European young people and was thinking how fortuntate I was to be an American and be free. As I watched them and learned from them, I realized that they were more free than I. I was seeing freedom as being free to travel, to own, to say; while they had given up the hopes that the world offers materially, and had become free to be God's people. I discovered that in reality they were far freer than I.

But let's not forget the woman of Samaria. While Jesus was conversing with her and offering her the living water, His disciples returned. As an illustration of the epitome of the problem, they marveled that he was talking to a Samaritan woman. They "besought him, saying, 'Rabbi, eat.' But He said to them, 'I have food to eat of which you do not know.' So the disciples said to one another, 'Has any one brought him food?' " (John 4:31–33). Having missed the message, they also missed the meaning. They were more concerned about food and whether He had eaten than they were about seeking the spiritual kingdom.

Like so many instances in the Scriptures, we, too, sometimes misunderstand the message and the messenger. It is necessary, therefore, to keep uppermost in mind that the realm of reality is the realm of the spiritual. Also, the material things of this world are secondary and they will pass away, unlike the spiritual things which will remain throughout eternity. Furthermore, we can hold fast to the idea that our worship is wasted unless it relates to the proper thing, because only true worship is the union of our individual spirits with God's spirit.

STUDY QUESTIONS

The Samaritans were half-Jews who had intermarried with the surrounding peoples during the Babylonian captivity. It was wrong for a Jew to marry a Gentile. Therefore, the Samaritans were outcasts from the Jews and each group hated the other. Since Jesus loved all men and was going to die for all men, He went through Samaria to give the Gospel to them, too. In His conversation with this Samaritan woman who had had five husbands, He told her a very important truth about God.

1. Tell the story of what happened with the woman. Why did Jesus ask for a drink? Where would He get "living water?"

2. What did the woman call Jesus in John 4, verse 9? Verse 19? Verse 29? Is there a development in her understanding?

3. In verse 24, Jesus said, "God is a Spirit." What does that mean? What does that tell us about God? How can God be everywhere?

4

God Is Person

How can we believe that God is a person? Have you ever touched God? The composite of who we are—of our emotional, physical, mental, and spiritual make-up is a reflection of what God is like. Those are facets of our personhood, of who we are as human beings. And the very essence of what forms that within us is God as a person. His characteristics ought to be the basis of our characteristics. In order to more fully understand God as a person, let's try to see it through the eyes of what man is like.

God: Like Man

In Genesis 1, we read that "Then God said, 'Let *us* make man in our image, after *our* likeness; and let *them* have dominion over the fish of the sea, and over the birds of the air, and over the cattle, and over all the earth, and over every creeping thing that creeps upon the earth.' So God created man in His own image, in the image of God He created him; male and female He created them" (1:26–27). Does anything strike you about the grammar in this passage? The pronouns referring to man change from singular to plural. Can God (the word in Hebrew is plural) speak in the singular and at the same time in the plural? Because he is the Trinity, He is one, yet He is three, the plurality of His being comes together in the Godhead. We can speak of God as "Him" and God can speak of His children and Himself as "us."

Notice also that it says, "God created man (singular), he created him (singular), male and female he created them (plural)." You see, the image of God is representative of the image of man, including male and female. This is how we are like God and created in His image. In Genesis 2, Moses states that God created female from the rib of male. God called her woman because she was taken from man. With this definition, we can understand the difference between the two. There is that element in man and woman which is like God. What do you think it is?

Obviously this can't be a physical likeness. More than the outward characteristic, we are concerned that God has placed within us a similarity with regard to image. How would you describe it? Perhaps we can define these qualities as personality, responsible being, the capacity for emotional relationships, spirit, soul, or the ability to make decisions.

Remember that to Noah, God said, "For behold, I will bring a flood of waters upon the earth, to destroy all flesh in which is the breath of life from under heaven; everything that is on earth shall die" (Gen. 6:17). And "everything on the dry land in whose nostrils was the breath of life died" (Gen. 7:22). In common with animals, we share certain life principles. We are, however, separated from animals by the very characteristics which we share with God and which make us persons. We have the ability to know what is in ourselves, the ability to learn, and the ability to make sense out of certain symbols whether written or spoken. Not only do we symbolize in that way, but also we symbolize in our behavior with body language or various gestures which indicate a wide range of emotions.

The emotional life that we live is also shared in common with what God is like. Because we're like God, we have the ability to relate to other people and to Him. Jesus says, "The father loves the Son," and we can see that within the godhead there is a relationship of love. It is part of God's design that love enters into human relationships, too, so that we learn to care about one another. We learn to laugh with one another, to enjoy one another's company, and to share in the tranquility of peaceful moments.

Going one step further, we know that our lives are different from the rest of Creation because of the decisions we make. We're entirely capable of deciding and willfully directing our lives. Psychologists take animals into their laboratories and chart out their behavior, learn about conditioned responses; and they have some success. Then they bring those results over to man, but they do not have the same success, because their definition of man has to be different than their definition of animals. Knowledge, emotional capacity, and will are different in each case. Therefore the initial understanding of what God is like as a person is most easily found when we analyze how He has made us in His own image.

When I was growing up, I feared God because in my mind He always seemed to allow things to go wrong for me. As a result, I learned to hide and to duck when anything adverse happened for fear I had misbehaved and all kinds of calamity would come down upon me. But I was missing what God was really like. I was not seeing that God is a perfect person who really cares, understands, and knows about all of us.

God: The I Am

Let's try to recognize man's characteristics in God. In the Old Testament God reveals himself to Moses very clearly. Until he made an error, Moses was one of the most successful people of his day. He was raised by Pharaoh's daughter, rose to a very powerful position in Egypt, and then he decided to take the deliverance of his people into his own hands. So he had to head out for the desert. "Now Moses was keeping the flock of his father-in-law, Jethro, the priest of Midian; and he led his flock to the west side of the wilderness, and came to Horeb, the mountain of God. And the angel of the Lord appeared to him in a flame of fire out of the midst of a bush; and he looked, and lo, the bush was burning, yet it was not consumed" (Exod. 3:1-2).

I've often wondered what it would have been like to have

been Moses. He had enjoyed all of the privileges and all of the luxuries of Egypt. And yet because of a mistake and resulting failure, he ended up in the desert, married to the daughter of a priest of another kind of religion and keeping sheep. How many times he must have thought about his former comfortable existence, the mistake he made, and re-analyzed what he would have done differently if given the opportunity! It reminds me of Joseph, who dreamed great dreams and instead of being the leader he thought he was to be, he was sold into slavery in Egypt, and ultimately sent to prison. The psalmist wrote that "His feet were hurt with fetters, his neck was put in a collar of iron; until what he had said came to pass the word of the Lord tested him" (Ps. 105:18–19).

Picture Moses, however, out in the wilderness taking care of his sheep, nothing left of life, no hope, no future. Then he sees a burning bush that isn't consumed by the fire. Except this was not just any fire. As he continued to watch it, the bush didn't burn up. Out of the bush came a voice, " 'Moses, Moses!' And he said, 'Here am I.' Then he said, 'Do not come near; put off your shoes from your feet, for the place on which you are standing is holy ground.' And he said, 'I am the God of your father, and God of Abraham, the God of Isaac, and the God of Jacob.' And Moses hid his face, for he was afraid to look at God" (Exod. 3:4–6). The brightness of the fire which was the appearance of God to Moses and the voice out of the past were overwhelming. I'm sure those years of failure came flooding back and Moses wondered why the Lord was there talking to him in such a spectacular way. Where had He been all those years that Moses really needed Him?

The Lord said, "I have seen the affliction of my people who are in Egypt, and have heard their cry because of their taskmasters; I know their sufferings, and I have come down to deliver them out of the hand of the Egyptians, and to bring them up out of that land to a good and broad land, a land flowing with milk and honey, to the place of the Canaanites, the Hittites, the Amorites, the Perizzites, the Hivites, and the Jebusites. And now, behold, the cry of the people of Israel has come to me, and I have seen the oppression with which the Egyptians oppress them. Come, I will send you to Pharaoh that you may bring forth my people, the sons of Israel, out of Egypt" (3:7–10). Can you imagine Moses' memory of the last time he faced Pharaoh? From forty years of watching bushes burn and winds blow and sheep eat, he had become incapable of really responding.

Moses said to God, "Who am I that I should go to Pharaoh and bring the sons of Israel out of Egypt?" God's answer is a very beautiful and short phrase, "I will be with you" (3:11–12). He doesn't tell Moses he is a failure, nor that he is a great man. Rather, he assures him that "I will be with you; and this shall be the sign for you, that I have sent you: when you have brought forth the people out of Egypt, you shall serve God upon this mountain" (3:12). It was a tremendous promise that Moses would return to the mountain with the people of Israel, but it wasn't much of a sign that could be carried along as a constant reminder of his task. It was simply a promise from God, "I will be with you." In this statement, you can see that God is a person. While He is not limited to a body, or to time or space or materialism; He is capable of fellowship with man.

Moses said to God, "If I come to the people of Israel and say to them, 'The God of your fathers has sent me to you,' and they ask me, 'What is his name?' what shall I say to them?" (3:13). Do you suppose a lot of people would ask the same question had they been given the task that God gave to Moses? I imagine that over the centuries because the course of events worsened, that the people of Israel were crying out for their God.

God answers His servant, "I am who I am. Say this to the people of Israel, 'I am has sent me to you' " (3:14). You see, because God is a person He can say "I am."

A song by Neil Diamond has lyrics which are startling in their meaning. "I am, I cried, and no one heard me. Not even the chair." This contemporary performer looks at this existential world and cries out with frustration over how he sees it. He sees the meaninglessness and the emptiness and the despair. He wants to assert who he is, but there is no one to answer. Not even the chair speaks in response to his person-hood. But he looks in the wrong direction to find the answer to "I am." God is the real one who can answer that question, the self-existent "I am who I am." Only because we're created in His image, can we, too, take our places next to the person of God.

God: I Respond

Let's explore God's conversation with Moses a bit further. The promise from God is earnestly stated, "I promise that I will bring you up out of the affliction of Egypt, to the land of the Canaanites, the Hittites, the Amorites, the Perizzites, the Hivites, and the Jebusites, a land flowing with milk and honey" (3:17). For Moses, however, this promise isn't enough. Through Moses' doubting eyes, God exhibits one more facet of his personhood—the capacity to make decisions. He is determined that Moses will bring the Israelites out of Egypt. Not believing his own ability to lead the people out of Egypt, Moses answers, "But behold, they will not believe me or listen to my voice, for they will say, 'The Lord did not appear to you'" (4:1).

Realizing that Moses needed more proof and encouragement, "The Lord said to him, 'What is that in your hand?' He said, 'A rod.' And he said, 'Cast it on the ground.' So he cast it on the ground, and it became a serpent; and Moses fled from it. But the Lord said to Moses. 'Put out your hand, and take it by the tail'—so he put out his hand and caught it, and it became a rod in his hand—'that they may believe that the Lord, the God of their fathers, the God of Abraham, the God of Isaac, and the God of Jacob, has appeared to you'" (4:2–5). God left Moses with more than a word and a promise of a return to the mountain. In addition, He took what Moses had and made it sufficient for what he needed to do. Moses' sin of unbelief brings further understanding of what God is like, and yet God remains compassionate and responsive.

Can you imagine Moses with a burning bush on one side and a snake on the other? What does he do? God had provided for every need, but still Moses wasn't satisfied. He said to the Lord, "Oh, my Lord, I am not eloquent, either heretofore or since thou hast spoken to thy servant; but I am slow of speech and of tongue" (4:10). I don't really think Moses had such a hard time talking, but I think he was still shuddering at the remembrance of how he had talked and failed so greatly before he entered the wilderness. Therefore, he told God that he couldn't even speak clearly enough to carry out the task. Again, think of the times he wished he could have replayed his previous years. But the Lord answered him, "Who has made man's mouth? Who makes him dumb, or deaf, or seeing, or blind? Is it not I, the Lord? Now therefore go, and I will be with your mouth and teach you what you shall speak" (4:11–12). Not only is God able to say that He will be with us, or to say, "I am." Nor is He only capable of transforming what is in his hand, but also He is able to put words into Moses' mouth. At the very heart of communication, God created the mouth and was able to help Moses use it.

Unfortunately, Moses still didn't believe God. He asked for someone else to be sent to help him. In God's answer to this request, we are able to determine that God also has a capacity for anger. "Then the anger of the Lord was kindled against Moses and he said, 'Is there not Aaron, your brother, the Levite?' " (4:14). Through Moses and the problems which resulted, we are able to see once again through the eyes of man a bit more of what God is like.

God: I Care

The story of Moses' brother as related in Numbers is another step in realizing that God is a person. "Miriam and Aaron spoke against Moses because of the Cushite woman whom he had married, for he had married a Cushite woman; and they said, 'Has the Lord indeed spoken only through Moses? Has he not spoken through us also?' " (12:1–2). Can you detect their jealousy? Moses has been speaking, he has gathered the people and organized them, and he has prepared them for entering into the land. Continually, Moses has been in the forefront. Miriam and Aaron are envious of his position. To gain retribution, they exploit his flaw, for he had married a foreigner. They don't criticize his leadership, but they do criticize his weak spot.

Five crucial words in this passage indicate to us another manifestation of God as a person. "And the Lord heard it" (12:2). Not only does He speak, but He also listens. "And suddenly the Lord said to Moses and to Aaron and Miriam, 'Come out, you three, to the tent of meeting.' And the three of them came out. And the Lord came down in a pillar of cloud, and stood at the door of the tent, and called Aaron and Miriam; and they both came forward. And he said, 'Hear my words: If there is a prophet among you, I the Lord make myself known to him in a vision, I speak with him in a dream. Not so with my servant Moses; he is entrusted with all my house. With him I speak mouth to mouth, clearly, and not in dark speech; and he beholds the form of the Lord. Why then were you not afraid to speak against my servant Moses?' " (12:4–8).

God responds in this situation as a person who cares. When Moses His servant is falsely and unjustly criticized, God enters and in this beautiful passage of Scripture defends His relationship with Moses. An additional picture of this association appears in Hebrews where we read that "Moses was faithful in all God's house as a servant, to testify to the things that were to be spoken later, but Christ was faithful over God's house as a son" (Heb. 3:5–6).

God: A Human Person

A final look at the person of God comes to us in the Gospel of John. "In the beginning was the Word, and the Word was with God, and the Word was God" (John 1:1). "The Word became flesh and dwelt among us, full of grace and truth; we have beheld his glory, glory as of the only Son from the Father" (1:14). Truth without grace can be destructive. Grace without truth can be misunderstood. The word of God comes to manifest what God is like, and in this way we can understand Him to be full of the "givingness"—the grace of God.

Moreover, it is clear that He is full of the revelation of God. These things we can see manifest in the *person* of God as Jesus Christ our Lord.

You see, we are created by God and all that we are is His work in our lives. Our personalities were created by Him. Our ability to make our own decisions is God-given. We are created in God's image and therefore our lives should mirror the essence of that image. Seeing God as a person enables us to formulate a more concrete understanding of the whole of His character.

STUDY QUESTIONS

1. If the image of God were simply defined as that which makes man qualitatively different from animal, what characteristic in us reflects God rather than animals?

2. List some ways that the fact that God is a person made a difference in His relationship with Moses.

3. How could this be illustrated in the lives of David, Daniel, and Mary?

4. How many of the emotions that we have are also attributed to God? How does this reflect on His and our personhood?

5

God Is Eternal

Our world changes on a regular basis. The economy fluctuates, governments rise and fall, and on a more personal level, our moods change frequently from happy to sad, gentle to angry, enthusiastic to uninterested, and back again. In contrast to all of this, we can recognize the constancy of God in our changing world.

God and Time

In his prayer in Psalm 102, the psalmist cries out to God, "Hear my prayer, O Lord; let my cry come to thee! Do not hide thy face from me in the day of my distress! Incline thy ear to me; answer me speedily in the day when I call!" (102:1–2). The honesty of praise and petition found in the Psalms is far more open and infinite with God than many of our empty demands on God's mercy. "My days pass away like smoke, and my bones burn like a furnace. My heart is smitten like grass, and withered; I forget to eat my bread. Because of my loud groaning my bones cleave to my flesh. I am like a vulture of the wilderness, like an owl of the waste places; I lie awake, I am like a lonely bird on the housetop. All the day my enemies taunt me, those who deride me use my name for a curse. For I eat ashes like bread, and mingle tears with my drink, because of thy indignation and anger; for thou hast taken me up and thrown me away. My days are like an evening shadow; I wither away like grass" (102:3–11).

David is explaining all of the agony through which he is going. His perspective of time is lost and he even forgets to eat. Relationships become unclear in his mind and he is stricken with loneliness. In the midst of his struggle he doesn't have any hope. He only sees that time is passing. Then he has reason to turn and look at God: "But thou, O Lord, art enthroned for ever; thy name endures to all generations. Thou wilt arise and have pity on Zion; it is the time to favor her; the appointed time has come" (102:12–13). He entreats God that now might be the time when Israel is restored to her joy and her fulfillment.

His discourse continues, "He has broken my strength in midcourse; he has shortened my days. 'O my God,' I say, 'take me not hence in the midst of my days, thou whose years endure throughout all generations!' " (102:23–24). He gains good perspective of the eternal God. "Of old thou didst lay the foundation of the earth, and the heavens are the work of thy hands. They will perish, but thou dost endure; they will all wear out like a garment. Thou changest them like raiment, and they pass away; but thou art the same, and thy years have no end. The children of thy servants shall dwell secure; their posterity shall be established before thee" (102:25–28). The psalmist sees that in the insecurity and struggle of his life, time continues to pass. All material things that he can claim to know will eventually fade out of existence. But for God, time is different because He is constant and consistent in all things.

God precedes the world. He is Creator of the world. The psalmist says that He wears the weather, and the changes that are a part of this world are like His garments. But He's not subject to the time. His years have no end. In Moses' psalm, he begins by saying "Lord, thou hast been our dwelling place in all generations. Before the mountains were brought forth, or ever thou hadst formed the earth and the world, from everlasting to everlasting thou art God" (90:1–2). It is difficult for us to understand what it is like not to have time. The longer man has lived, the greater has become our capacity to divide time into smaller sections. All of us have watched the Olympics and seen how they can time swimming races down to a hundreth of a second. We have learned to divide time into smaller and smaller and smaller units.

We can be encouraged that God is exactly the opposite from the world's concept of time. He is not limited by it, yet He works within time in our world. Paul illustrates the Lord's relationship to time so beautifully in the first chapter of Ephesians. "Blessed be the God and Father of our Lord Jesus Christ, who has blessed us in Christ with every spiritual blessing in the heavenly places, even as he chose us in him before the foundation of the world, that we should be holy and blameless before him. He destined us in love to be his sons through Jesus Christ, according to the purpose of his will, to the praise of his glorious grace which he freely bestowed on us in the Beloved" (Eph. 1:3–6). In this passage, Paul shows the work of the Father in regard to our salvation. That work is not something that just happens in the midst of time, but it began far before time. It happened before God even laid the foundation of the world, and marked out those that were to be His for the purpose that we should be holy and blameless before Him.

Having created for us a new life, He purposed that this might be accomplished through Jesus Christ, according to the purpose of His will to the praise of His glorious grace. This plan that He started before the foundation of the world is worked out during the time in which we live. "For he has made known to us in all wisdom and insight the mystery of his will, according to his purpose which he set forth in Christ as a plan for the fulness of time, to unite all things in him, things in heaven and things on earth" (1:9–10). You see, God began acting on our behalf before He ever created the world. And then He entered the world in the form of Jesus Christ to provide redemption and forgiveness of sins so that when time is completed all things might be united and brought back together in Him.

God and Aging

God does not age. He acts before time exists; He acts through time, and then when time is brought to completion, again He is acting in bringing forth a group of people like Himself as trophies of His grace for all eternity. This is a mystery and we don't begin to understand it. We see all things in the perspective of consequential action. We see time as linear. We see it progressing from a beginning to an end. But God is far greater, far different than that. Notice the great commission that He gives to us in Matthew 28. "All authority in heaven and on earth has been given to me. Go therefore and make disciples of all nations, baptizing them in the name of the Father and of the Son and of the Holy Spirit, teaching them to observe all that I have commanded you; and lo, I am with you always, to the close of the age" (28:18–20). His promise to the disciples is that wherever they go and whatever they do as they carry out His commission, He is with them throughout all of time.

Often we are caught in the inability to do what we would like to do because we grow old and are subject to time. Our Savior and our heavenly Father, however, are not that way. The writer of Hebrews finishes his Book with a series of exhortations about the relationship of the saints. "Remember your leaders, those who spoke to you the word of God; consider the outcome of their life, and imitate their faith. Jesus Christ is the same yesterday and today and for ever" (13:7–8). Those who first heard the message from Christ were a demonstration of His power. Their lives produced the very results that they're teaching. Now, as the writer of Hebrews writes to this people who are undergoing persecution, for whom the struggle is going to get worse, he encourages them by saying that Jesus Christ is the same now and forever. He is not subject to the process of aging, nor is He subject to the process of change. But He is consistently the same because He is the eternal one, part of the eternal godhead.

God and Change

The eternal nature of God leads us to a new understanding of what He is like. He is without change. There's a beautiful illustration of this in the last of the Old Testament prophets. "Behold, I send my messenger to prepare the way before me, and the Lord whom you seek will suddenly come to his temple; the messenger of the covenant in whom you can delight, behold, he is coming, says the Lord of hosts. But who can endure the day of his coming, and who can stand when he appears? For he is like a refiner's fire and like fullers' soap; he will sit as a refiner and purifier of silver, and he will purify the sons of Levi and refine them like gold and silver, till they present right offerings to the Lord" (Mal. 3:1–3).

God speaks of that day when His messenger will come and when the judgment will come. Israel missed this, because when John the Baptist preached of the judgment, they were looking for the kingdom and they wondered what he was saying. "For I the Lord do not change; therefore you, O sons of Jacob, are not consumed" (3:6). The struggle of Israel in sin often caused God to look upon the people in judgment. Often these conflicts caused him to act upon Israel with discipline. He is faithful, though, to the covenant throughout all of the time of Israel, because He does not change. Therefore Israel is not consumed. The reality of Israel's presence in the world today and its dominance in every foreign policy in the world is further illustration of the unchanging nature of God, that He keeps His covenant, that He is faithful to His Word, and is always consistent with His people.

This eternal consistency of God has led James to write the first chapter of his epistle to a troubled group of people, "Do not be deceived, my beloved brethren. Every good endowment and every perfect gift is from above, coming down from the Father of lights with whom there is no variation or shadow due to change. Of his own will he brought us forth by the word of truth that we should be a kind of first fruits of his creatures" (James 1:16–18). As James talks about the struggles of facing trials and temptations in this world, and then speaks even more deeply of the temptation that comes from within ourselves, he says that we are to understand that God is constant in His goodness toward us. Every good and perfect gift *is* from above, coming down from a Father in whom there is absolutely no change. There is not even change in shadow, because He is unfailingly working toward us in goodness.

Immutability sometimes is interpreted as immobility. Many people perceive that God is unchanging and therefore assume He is unable to act. But this is not the case. In fact, the Old Testament and the New Testament are full of illustrations where God acts in perfect consistency with his character as He responds to us. A fascinating picture is in Exodus 32 of a God who seemingly changes but when we look carefully, we find that He is the unchanging God. Moses had delivered the people from Egypt, had brought them to the mountain, and there they had made their commitment to Him in regard to their covenant. Moses returned from the mountain to gain from God the law. "When the people saw that Moses delayed to come down from the mountain, the people gathered themselves together to Aaron, and said to him, 'Up, make us gods, who shall go before us; as for this Moses, the man who brought us up out of the land of Egypt, we do not know what has become of him" (32:1).

Fascinatingly enough, the people did not know who had delivered them from Egypt. They thought it was Moses, and when Moses was gone, God was gone. They had missed the message, although they had heard and followed the messenger. So while Moses is away, the people of Israel ask for a new god. They want a god who this time can take them on to the next step in the process of deliverance out of Egypt.

Aaron becomes a partner with the Israelites. They make a molten calf and set it up to worship. "And they rose up early on the morrow, and offered burnt offerings and brought peace offerings; and the people sat down to eat and drink, and rose up to play" (32:6). This attitude starts with idolatry, continues to celebration, and ultimately produces immorality because the words "to play" are translated as a kind of behavior that goes against the very nature and character of God.

While this idol worship continues, the Lord says to Moses

in the mountain," 'Go down; for your people, whom you brought up out of the land of Egypt, have corrupted themselves; they have turned aside quickly out of the way which I commanded them; they have made for themselves a molten calf, and have worshiped it and sacrificed to it, and said, "These are your gods, O Israel, who brought you up out of the land of Egypt!" ' And the Lord said to Moses, 'I have seen this people, and behold, it is a stiff-necked people; now therefore let me alone, that my wrath may burn hot against them and I may consume them; but of you I will make a great nation' " (32:7–10).

Do you see how God responds in perfect consistency with His character? He is unchanging in His hatred for sin. As Israel turns to idolatry, God responds in anger and in judgment upon the people. Then Moses steps in to that beautiful place of mediation and he intercedes for his people before God. The people who Moses has brought out of the land of Egypt are not his people. "O Lord, why does thy wrath burn hot against thy people, whom thou hast brought forth out of the land of Egypt with great power and with a mighty hand? Why should the Egyptians say, 'With evil intent did he bring them forth, to slay them in the mountains, and to consume them from the face of the earth?' Turn from thy fierce wrath, and repent of this evil against thy people. Remember Abraham, Isaac, and Israel, thy servants, to whom thou didst swear by thine own self, and didst say to them, 'I will multiply your descendants as the stars of heaven, and all this land that I have promised I will give to your descendants, and they shall inherit it for ever.' " (32:11–13).

The key idea in this interchange is "the Lord repented of the evil which he thought to do to his people" (32:14). The word "repented" here means to change His mind. It is not that God has changed it, but it is that He has again been unchanging and consistent in the faithfulness of His person. As Moses intercedes for his people on the basis of the name and the promise of God, God responds to his faith and changes the judgment that He had just made.

Once I had a boss, and when we employees entered the

office in the morning, we checked with his secretary to see if this was a day to talk to him or avoid him. On some days he would respond favorably to almost anything we could ask him. On other days he would reject immediately even the best of suggestions. We learned through the eyes of his secretary, to live with the inconsistency. But God is not that way. He has always been and always will be the same. We can rest in that relationship because He is eternally unchanging.

God is eternal. God is unchanging. God is infinite in His personhood and perfectly consistent at all times. Therefore we can always trust Him to be against evil, to respond to faith, to place His blessing upon His people, and to help us accomplish all for which we are willing to believe Him.

STUDY QUESTIONS

Some people have looked at this world and said that it is always changing. It is never the same. Some things, though, never change and we can always depend on them.

1. Can you think of some things in this world that do not seem to change?

2. What things change according to Psalm 102:25–26? What doesn't change? What difference does that make?

3. When Israel was very sinful, God had to punish her, but He never destroyed her. Why not? (Genesis 28:13–15 and Malachi 3:6).

4. In a world where everything changes, we are always faced with various temptations. What does this mean to the Christian who knows the unchanging God? (James 1:17–18). Our world will constantly change. Will you react as one who depends on an unchanging God?

5. All of creation is growing old because death is on the way. God will not die and therefore does not change. How does this affect you?

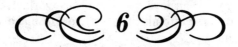

God Is Love

For most of us, love is that warm fuzzy feeling that we have some of the time about some people. It often happens in marriage. Frequently it happens in courtship. Too often it happens outside marriage. Rarely is it analyzed or thought about very much. There are days when we have it for a lot of people and there are days when we don't feel anything at all. Emotions, warmth of relationships with people, and sexual feelings cause the warm feeling, and that's not bad. But our world makes a mistake about calling that warm fuzzy feeling love.

We talk about a different concept when we talk about the love of God. Other qualities enhance the love which God shows for his children. It is that love which is undeserved—a gift freely bestowed. Eternal and consistent best describe it.

Paul speaks of God's love in the first chapter of Philippians. Written to one of his supporting churches, this epistle chronicles a lifestyle based upon a poured-out life. "I thank my God in all my remembrance of you, always in every prayer of mine for you all making my prayer with joy, thankful for your partnership in the gospel from the first day until now. And I am sure that he who began a good work in you will bring it to completion at the day of Jesus Christ. It is right for me to feel thus about you all, because I hold you in my heart, for you are all partakers with me of grace, both in my imprisonment and in the defense and confirmation of the gospel" (1:3–7). Reading Paul's statement could cause a bit of a warm fuzzy feeling. Paul was supported by this church, and he had just received another contribution. His feelings toward the people of Philippi were very strong. Because they supported him, he felt that they were an integral part of his work. He knew that God would do for them all that He had promised and all that He had begun.

Paul continued his prayer of thanksgiving, "For God is my witness, how I yearn for you all with the affection of Christ Jesus. And it is my prayer that your love may abound more and more, with knowledge and all discernment, so that you may approve what is excellent, and may be pure and blameless for the day of Christ, filled with the fruits of righteousness which come through Jesus Christ, to the glory and praise of God" (1:8–11). Pay particular attention to the phrase, "that your love may abound more and more, with knowledge and all discernment" (1:9). Every nice deed is not necessarily an act of love. The love Paul is talking about is a carefully worked out kind of love, carefully defined and thought through. It is a love that grows as it is better understood, and as it grows it approves what is excellent. It is the kind of love that fills us with the fruits of righteousness.

The opposite is the kind of love propagated in our materialistic world. We are easily caught in the love of things. Parents have come to my office not understanding what was wrong with their child. Their son or daughter in college would be flunking out, fooling with drugs, and in deep trouble. "We gave our children everything," they would say, "and they never seemed thankful or never seemed to enjoy what we provided for them." Clearly, these parents had mistaken doing things for loving their children. So often it is, for example, "Daddy, will you play ball with me?" And the response comes back, "Here's five dollars. Go buy another baseball." Literally, these people have given their kids everything and mistaken that for love. But in actuality, they were almost destroying the young ones, because they were withholding the most important thing from their kids—parental love; at the same time they were providing all sorts of things that the kids never needed, wanted, or even enjoyed. Sadly enough, these people had loved without discernment, without knowledge, and without understanding. In fact, they loved their habits and hobbies more than they loved their kids. They gave their children things, while they read the newspaper or kept on working in the kitchen.

God's Love—A Love that Serves

The love spoken of in Scripture is exactly the opposite. The perfect illustration of this kind of love can be found in the second chapter of Philippians. "Let each of you look not only to his own interests, but also to the interests of others. Have this mind among yourselves, which is yours in Christ Jesus, who, though he was in the form of God, did not count equality with God a thing to be grasped, but emptied himself, taking the form of a servant, being born in the likeness of men. And being found in human form he humbled himself and became obedient unto death, even death on a cross" (2:4–8). Paul says that this is the way we ought to think. God loved the world so much that He gave His only Son, His Son who possessed all that God was.

Let me illustrate this passage of Scripture. If you are secure in your position, you don't have to wear a particular uniform. If a physician or a minister has to wear his white coat or his collar so everyone will know who he is, his occupational capacity may be questionable. It seems as if his security comes from his uniform, not his ability. Paul is saying that Jesus was so much like God he didn't need to wear a uniform to prove it; He could pour Himself out of the godly form and take on a new form—the form of a servant. Being in the outward form like a man, He grew up and went through the experiences of humanity. He humbled Himself and became obedient even unto death.

This kind of sacrificial love is also illustrated for us in the thirteenth chapter of John. Jesus makes His passover meal with the disciples a living object lesson. Here is told the story of Jesus' last night on earth. Imagine what it would have been like to be there. I travel a lot and there are many times when I sit down with the family and make all the arrangements for the time I'll be gone. I assign various responsibilities to my daughters, so that everything continues to function well. In a small way, I think that Jesus, knowing He would die the next day and that His whole life's work is tied up in these twelve men, wants to spend the last hours teaching them all that they need to know in order to carry on His work. The arrangements are made for the Passover meal to be served. This is the only recorded sacrifice that Jesus offered. In anticipation of the meal, He sent some of the disciples ahead to prepare the feast.

While making the proper preparations, the disciples have become concerned about which one of them could be considered the greatest. Because of the ensuing discussion, they had rushed to the upper room, each of them eager to take his place at Jesus' right and at his left. By human standards, those places were reserved for the greatest of the disciples. As they arrive, I think that John sits on the right side and Judas on the left. They recline at the table and, assuming that they're all right-handed, if John leans back to talk to Jesus, then he is on the right. Judas dips water in the same bowl with Jesus, so he would be on the left. During the meal, the rest of the disciples probably begin to debate what right John has to be next to the Master. At the same time Jesus is thinking that He only has a few more hours and then the disciples are on their own. He already knows that they will deny Him, and He already knows that they will feel defeated.

Can you catch the two totally different perspectives happening in the room? In the hurry for seats, apparently no one was willing to be a servant and perform the ritual of washing the feet. It would be like me inviting you over to dinner at our house and after greeting you but before taking your coat, saying, "We're just about ready to eat, why not sit down here," and then never taking your coat. One of the rituals of hospitality is lacking. You see, everyone at the Passover knew the foot washing should be performed, but no one was willing to be the first to mention it, or to offer to do it. So as the meal progresses, Jesus in an object lesson does what Paul describes in Philippians 2. He took off the robe that showed Him to be Lord and Master. He put on a new robe of a different form, for He girded Himself with a towel. He picked up the basin and did what none of the disciples would do.

Notice the first verse, "Now before the feast of the passover, when Jesus knew that his hour had come to depart out of this world to the Father, having loved his own who were in the world, he loved them to the end" (John 13:1). He has loved them, He loves them right up to the end, and He is love. When you read on to the end of the chapter, you find Jesus saying, "Little children, yet a little while I am with you. You will seek me; and as I said to the Jews so now I say to you, 'Where I am going you cannot come.' A new commandment I give to you, that you love one another; even as I have loved you, that you also love another. By this all men will know that you are my disciples, if you have love for one another" (13:33–35). Here is stated the primary sign of Christianity— that we love one another. Jesus is saying, "All men will know you belong to Me if you obey this commandment, because sacrificial love is contrary to man's way of loving."

God's Love—A Love that Is Undeserved

I was teaching this lesson in a college classroom one time and stated that God's love does not come naturally. A young man who rarely seemed to be awake in class raised his hand and said, "Dr. Hook, that's not true. This kind of love is among friends all the time. We love one another sacrificially." I asked him if that feeling of love felt among companions was extended to the administration as well. At that point, he didn't want to continue the subject, because he was attending school in the sixties when there was a tremendous feeling of rebellion toward the administration. When students were pulling together, they learned to love each other. They contained their love within their group and made no move to extend it beyond their tightly knit circle.

You see, God so loved the world, not just His buddies, not

just His roommates, not just the Trinity, but the *world*, that He gave His Son. His Son loved mankind so much that He took off the robes, took the form of a servant, and washed the disciples' feet. That kind of love doesn't come naturally in our "grab all the gusto you can" world.

When our daughters were small, often they would wake up during the night and cry. I developed a system of rolling over and hitting my wife in the back with my elbow so she could get up and take care of the babies. Then I would lie there in bed feeling guilty as I thought about what "unselfish" love I had. I loved my children so much that I would wake up my wife so she could take care of them. Yet she very beautifully loved the kids in a sacrificial manner. She always got up and took care of them. One night during the summer I heard a baby cry. I started to roll over and nudge my wife when I realized that it wasn't one of our girls. The windows were open and a neighbor baby was crying. So I went back to sleep. And the next morning I began to struggle a bit with the question. When we get up and take care of our children during the night, is it so they can go back to sleep, or to get them quiet so we can go back to sleep? In a sense parental love is an unselfish love, except it is love for my kids. It really doesn't extend to the neighbors' young ones when they cry. Therefore while parental love may be unselfish in some ways, in others it is very selfish. But you see, God's love is not based on our merits. It is undeserved and yet constant for all of us.

God's Love—A Love that Disciplines

The love of God not only serves and is undeserved, but it also has an unusual dimension. It does the hard part; it disciplines. In Hebrews 12 we can see this concept at work. Persecution plagued the church. People were struggling with persecution for their faith in Christ. Hebrews is written partially to convince people that there might be no other way to live life if you know Christ. It encourages us to persevere in all things, "looking to Jesus the pioneer and perfecter of our faith, who for the joy that was set before him endured the cross, despising the shame, and is seated at the right hand of

God. Consider him who endured from sinners such hostility against himself, so that you may not grow weary or faint-hearted. In your struggle against sin you have not yet resisted to the point of shedding your blood. And have you forgotten the exhortation which addressed you as sons?—'My son, do not regard lightly the discipline of the Lord, nor lose courage when you are punished by him. For the Lord disciplines him whom he loves, and chastises every son whom he receives.' It is for discipline that you have to endure. God is treating you as sons; for what son is there whom his father does not discipline? If you are left without discipline, in which all have participated, then you are illegitimate children and not sons" (12:2–8).

Easy love gives the son five dollars and tells him to go buy another baseball. Easy love diverts a child's attention, rather than dealing with what he has been doing wrong. Easy love buys a new television to babysit the children, rather than teaching them how to live in reality. Tough love does what is best for the one that is loved even if it is temporarily painful to self or the one receiving love.

There are many perspectives to the question, "Why is there so much suffering?" One of them is the result of what man brings upon himself. Another perspective is that suffering is characteristic of a world ruled by sin.

A third perspective is that God is involved and He uses the struggling and the suffering as part of His training, part of discipling His children. There's no way that a person gets strong lying in bed, nor does he strengthen his muscles by sitting in a chair. Growth and strength come out of the labor of working. Growth of character comes out of the struggles and the hard times which arise from a variety of circumstances. Learning not to do that which is wrong comes out of the hurt that comes with disobedience. You see, God as a loving Father loves us so much that He disciplines us. It is a love with knowledge and with understanding. The discipline is never more than we're able to take, but it is always enough to keep us learning, to keep us tuned in.

God's Love—The Love that Motivates

Another dimension of God's love is revealed to us in First
Corinthians 13. This familiar passage is not so directly concerned with defining love as it is with describing what God's
love is like when it is in operation in the church. After defining and describing the gifts of the Spirit in chapter 12, Paul
wrote, "I will show you a still more excellent way" (1 Cor.
12:31). The key to serving God within the church is through
our gifts. But a higher way is service motivated by love.

The opening three verses are particularly illustrative of
this. Paul hypothetically describes the value of using our gifts
without love being the motivation. In each supposition he
starts with the normal description of the gift and then moves
to an extreme description. Each time he concludes that love-
less use of gifts is only emptiness.

Watch how this develops. If I speak with the tongues of
men (the regular gift) and even of angels (the extremity of
speaking), I am a noisy gong or a clanging symbol. And if I
have prophetic powers (the regular gift) and understand all
mysteries and all knowledge (the extreme gift) and if I have all
faith (regular gift) so as to remove mountains (the extremity),
and have not love I am nothing. And if I give away all that I
have (regular gift) and if I deliver my body to be burned
(extremity), but have not love I am nothing.

I often wonder how many pastors would be happy to have a
church full of people who spoke eloquently, who understood
deeply, who prayed effectively, and who gave sacrificially.
Would they really be satisfied? Paul says that such a church
without love is really nothing. Probably this is why, in Revelation 2, the warning to the church of Ephesus which has lost its
first love, is among the most severe warnings in the Book.
Love is that attribute which transforms an action into visible
manifestation of God and shows what He is like.

This is the heart of understanding one of the best known
verses of all of Scripture, "For God so loved the world that he
gave his only begotten Son" (John 3:16). It is God's love that
moves Him to action, and it is the Cross which becomes the
symbol of that love. In terms of our faith, it is the church

which becomes the instrument of that love to a world which does not know God.

Going one step further, we need to understand that this kind of love is not only that which motivates, it is also an action that can be seen. Because love is a verb, it can be known by what it does. Therefore, "Love is patient and kind; love is not boastful; it is not arrogant or rude. Love does not insist on its own way; it is not irritable or resentful; it does not rejoice at wrong, but rejoices in right. Love bears all things, believes all things, hopes all things, endures all things" (1 Cor. 13:4–7). Love is a way of doing those things; it is not an emotion that causes the fuzzy feelings. Because it is a way of doing things, it exemplifies the eternal relationship of the Trinity. The Father loves the Son and therefore love outlasts time. Love becomes greater than all of the gifts because it is the eternal God-like relationship that we will share.

STUDY QUESTIONS

1. God's love is very different from man's. Show some ways that it is different in Luke 6:32–36. Can you think of some other ways? How does John 13 and Jesus washing the disciples' feet illustrate this?

2. In First Corinthians 13, we have a description of God's love. Make a list of things that love does.

3. Why has a cross become a sign of God's love? (John 3:16; 1 John 3:16)

4. What are some ways that we can show love to others?

7

God Is Holy

The loveliness of a bride is a wonderful sight to behold. I have never performed a wedding for a homely bride. The brides may not always be beautiful before or after the wedding. I've sat in my office for pre-marital counseling occasionally thinking that this one will break the record. Somehow, though, the bride is always radiant in her lovely dress when she comes down the aisle on her father's arm. She glows as she enjoys the splendor of her day.

God's holiness can make us beautiful through purification just as the bride is beautiful. The work of the living presence of God in our lives has a transforming effect upon a sinner's life. However, sometimes the holiness of God scares us even though it shouldn't since almost everything in this world needs to be purified before it can be made lovely. Consider, if you will, this passage of Scripture, "Worship the Lord in the beauty of holiness" (Ps. 29:2, KJV). When we come to see God in His beauty, it is then that we also see Him in His holiness. The glow of who He is begins to purify us and we begin to radiate a holiness that is miraculous and beautiful.

The Concept of God's Holiness

The Old Testament prophet, Haggai, asks two interesting questions about God's holiness as he rebukes Israel's sin in

61

failing to rebuild the temple. "If one carries holy flesh in the skirt of his garment, and touches with his skirt bread, or pottage, or wine, or oil, or any kind of food, does it become holy? The priests answered, 'No' " (Hag. 2:12). Haggai then asks, "If one who is unclean by contact with a dead body touches any of these, does it become unclean?" (2:13). And the answer is "yes." Remember that the way of this world is that clean things touched by the dirt of the world become dirty, but a holy object cannot cleanse something else. God's holiness is different because His touch on our lives makes us clean.

Think back to the story in John 4 about the woman at the well. When the disciples returned to the well with food, they couldn't believe that Jesus was talking to a Samaritan woman. They feared that He had become defiled by drinking from her cup. In reality, those men had misunderstood what had happened. You see, the emphasis wasn't so much that Jesus might have been defiled, but more importantly, the woman had been made clean by His touch. In one short and meaningful conversation with the Lord, her entire lifestyle had changed. At first she was not highly regarded in the town, or by the disciples, but she finished her encounter with Jesus ready to drink of the living water. She was now able to reflect God's holiness in her life, a possibility she had never even considered before.

The Contradiction to God's Holiness

How do you perceive the holiness, the righteousness of God? Is it a concept we accept on faith, or something that we can fully understand? Often we face a dilemma in our spiritual lives because we can't understand the perfection of God's holiness. Let's go back to Habakkuk for a while. This book in the Old Testament is a good insight into the holiness of God and man's problems about it. Habakkuk is a prophet at a time when there is tremendous sin and disobedience in the land. Look closely at the conversation he has with God and notice what is happening here. "O Lord, how long shall I cry for help, and thou wilt not hear? Or cry to thee 'Violence?' and thou wilt not save? Why dost thou make me see wrongs and look upon trouble? Destruction and violence are before me; strife and contention arise. So the law is slacked and justice never goes forth. For the wicked surround the righteous, so justice goes forth perverted" (1:2-4). What can we know about Habakkuk from these comments? He is impatient, frustrated, negative, compassionate, idealistic. We can also learn something about his country. He is living in a land plagued by a lot of disobedience and violence. Perhaps he is wondering why trouble is coming his way when so many others are acting worse than he is, and they don't seem to be suffering any hardships.

His relationship with God is important to define too. We see him asking God whether or not He cares and if so, where is He every time Habakkuk needs him. In fact Habakkuk acts as if he is the righteous person and God is the unrighteous one. Notice how this questioning tone changes in the next few verses as God responds to Habakkuk's accusations.

God answers his question, "Look among the nations, and see; wonder and be astounded. For I am doing a work in your days that you would not believe if told. For lo, I am rousing the Chaldeans, that bitter and hasty nation, who march through the breadth of the earth, to seize habitations not their own. Dread and terrible are they; their justice and dignity proceed from themselves. Their horses are swifter than leopards, more fierce than the evening wolves; their horsemen press proudly on. Yea, their horsemen come from afar; they fly like an eagel swift to devour. They all come for violence; terror of them goes before them. They gather captives like sand. At kings they scoff, and of rulers they make sport. They laugh at every fortress, for they heap up earth and take it" (1:5-10).

Look at how God answers Habakkuk. He says He *knows* how much violence there is in the land; it is in His perfect plan for Israel to be disciplined. But first, there is a small nation to the north which is a dread and terrible nation. They're going to come down and wipe things out, and this siege will also include Israel.

Once again, Habakkuk begins to speak. "Art thou not from everlasting, O Lord my God, my Holy One? We shall not die. O Lord, thou hast ordained them as a judgment; and thou, O Rock, hast established them for chastisement." Note the change of tone here: "Thou who art of purer eyes than to behold evil and canst not look on wrong, why dost thou look on faithless men, and art silent when the wicked swallows up the man more righteous than he?" (1:12–13). What is Habakkuk saying? He seems to change his approach somewhat, doesn't he? First he is concerned about the nation's survival, and then he becomes accusing again. In a way, he has manipulated God into a corner so that only one decision is possible. Habakkuk's definition of holiness really does not allow God to do what God has said He plans to do. Because he disagrees with God's kind of solution, he accuses God of doing an unholy thing. He feels that God just can't look upon evil; how then can God deal with the evil in this world? Is our concept of holiness ever like Habakkuk's? Do we ever have tunnel vision upwards in thinking of God's righteousness?

This interesting conversation with God continues and the prophet says, "I will take my stand to watch, and station myself on the tower, and look forth to see what he will say to me, and what I will answer concerning my complaint" (2:1). You see, he is honest enough to know that he is putting God on the spot; he wonders what the Lord will do next.

God graciously answers the impatient prophet. "Write the vision; make it plain upon tablets, so he may run who reads it. For still the vision awaits its time; it hastens to the end—it will not lie. If it seem slow, wait for it; it will surely come, it will not delay. Behold, he whose soul is not upright in him shall fail, but the righteous shall live by his faith" (2:2–4). God's answer to Habakkuk explains that the prophet must have patience and trust in God's wisdom. In the middle of what is happening around him, Habakkuk doesn't understand the course of events. But because of God's concern for his welfare, Habakkuk will come to understand the reasons behind God's actions.

In the following paragraphs, God explains that justice comes with time. You reap what you sow. Can you see that God doesn't favor the unrighteous? "Woe to him who gets evil gain for his house, to set his nest on high, to be safe from the reach of harm! You have devised shame to your house by cutting off many peoples; you have forfeited your life. For the stone will cry out from the wall, and the beam from the woodwork respond" (2:9–11). There are no secure little suburbs where you can get away with unrighteousness. This example continues in the next few verses. "Woe to him who builds a town with blood, and founds a city on iniquity! Behold, is it not from the Lord of hosts that peoples labor only for fire, and nations weary themselves for nought? For the earth will be filled with the knowledge of the glory of the Lord, as the waters cover the sea" (2:12–14). How many nations do you know of that are built on blood? Is this something that is unique to Habakkuk's day? Unfortunately some of the more powerful nations in the world today are built that way. But we know it is not with the blessing of God in His holiness.

In God's infinite wisdom, He tells us that it isn't from Him that people labor only for fire. Such an investment of time and energy won't pay off because nothing can be gained from it. How busy we can get wanting to destroy the nation, and many other things, I might add, that God is going to deal with in His own time! If the Lord delays His coming awhile, those nations won't get away with doing evil. No nation in history has succeeded yet in doing so.

To make this graphic, God takes them to the ultimate absurdity—man's creation of his own gods. "What profit is an idol when its maker has shaped it, a metal image, a teacher of lies? For the workman trusts in his own creation when he makes dumb idols! Woe to him who says to a wooden thing, Awake; to a dumb stone, Arise! Can this give revelation? Behold, it is overlaid with gold and silver, and there is no breath at all in it" (2:18–19). He persists, saying that it doesn't do any good to make for youself little idols that can't speak or breathe.

Can you follow the conversation? The Lord tells Habakkuk to trust His holy design because the wicked won't get away with their harmful ways. You may see it as unjust because it looks as if evil will prevail at any time. But in the long run, God promises that there will be justice. The climactic assertion of the book follows, "But the Lord is in his holy temple; let all the earth keep silence before him" (2:20). The real answer is that Habakkuk is seeing the work of a holy God. What he needs is the patience and trust to believe that God knows what He is doing, and that what He is doing is right. Like Habakkuk, we need to keep still and recognize God's careful design for our lives. Where is His holy temple? It is the universe, and many experiences and instances attest to the fact that a holy God is at work. Therefore, *we* don't have to go around playing God. At times, like Habakkuk, we want to cry out to God for His indifference to the evil that surrounds us. We come up with a solution, and want some action from heaven to support it. But man's solution is pitiful in comparison to that of a holy God's. In reality we can be confident of what God is going to do.

The Confidence in God's Holiness

You see, the holiness of God is not something awesome to be feared. It is one of the beautiful confidences of the believer. The man who trusts in God can have the assurance that ultimately whatever happens will be right and just. Because of that reality, we can wait. Remember Isaiah's comment in the year that King Uzziah died. This was a time of great discouragement for the prophet. The faithful king is dead and Isaiah is probably very mournful, but now God chooses to reveal his holiness to Isaiah. "I saw the Lord sitting upon a throne, high and lifted up; and his train filled the temple" (Isa. 6:1). Do you recall how Isaiah reacted? He said, "Woe is me! For I am lost: for I am a man of unclean lips" (6:5). He felt undeserving of being in God's presence. Did God tell him that he was right and ask him to leave? Not at all. Rather, He sent an angel to take a coal from the altar and touch Isaiah's lips. And then

God asked him who should be sent to make the people of that nation understand Him. The positive response comes back, "Here am I! Send me" (6:8). He started out discouraged, realized his sin and inadequacy, and ended up as God's messenger.

The holiness of God often can be a mirror where we see what we are like. There is comfort in our fear of God's righteousness because He will turn that fear into opportunity. Isaiah entered the presence of God fearing the circumstances, but he left it willing to serve the Master as a purified messenger. We don't need to fear God. We do need to recognize what we are, and allow Him to work in our lives. Then God will turn us around so that we can manifest what He is like. When He changes the way we think, He starts to manifest Himself in the way we live.

The standard of holiness which God sets is important for us to realize. We cannot escape it if we truly strive to know what God is like. The example is clarified in Leviticus 11:44. "For I am the Lord your God; consecrate yourselves therefore, and be holy, for I am holy. You shall not defile yourselves with any swarming thing that crawls upon the earth. For I am the Lord who brought you up out of the land of Egypt, to be your God; you shall therefore be holy, for I am holy." There is a sense of "I am, therefore you shall be" that God presents to us. He gives us a positive and plausible course to follow.

God's example of holiness is further echoed for us in First Peter 1:13–16. "Therefore gird up your minds, be sober, set your hope fully upon the grace that is coming to you at the revelation of Jesus Christ. As obedient children, do not be conformed to the passions of your former ignorance, but as he who called you is holy, be holy yourselves in all your conduct; since it is written, 'You shall be holy, for I am holy.' " Not only does the Lord set the example, but He also offers suggestions for the practical working out of it. He speaks of hope, obedience, and holiness in this passage. He urges us as His children to prepare ourselves, our souls, and our bodies to do away with former ignorance. In so doing, we shall be holy because He is holy.

The Cleansing Based on God's Holiness

The very practical implications of this are brought out in John's first letter, which is the mirror image of the Gospel of John. In the gospel, he says that these things "are written that you may believe that Jesus is the Christ" (John 20:31). In John's gospel, he writes how we might know in order to have life through believing; in the epistle, he turns it around and says how we can know that we have eternal life because we have believed. One checks up on why we believe; the other checks up on how we know we have believed. Of course the answer is that our lives have been transformed in the way we walk, in the way we love because of God, and in the life we have in Christ.

The reality of God's holiness helps us to understand the difference between darkness and light in the Biblical sense. The key passage in regard to the holiness of God is the following principle. "This is the message we have heard from him and proclaim to you, that God is light and in him is no darkness at all" (1 John 1:5). The concept is built on two symbols, light and darkness. The choosing of these symbols is very carefully done, because the two cannot coexist. If there is light, there is no darkness, and the opposite of this is true also.

We sometimes see light as relative, there is a dim light or a bright light. In the absolute sense, though, there is light or there isn't. If there is not, then there is darkness. God is like that. There is direction, there is purity, there is understanding and visibility of where we ought to be and where we ought to go when God is there. We know that when God is not there, only the darkness prevails. You see, there is no beauty in darkness. There is only fear and uncertainty, lack of direction, lack of meaning, and lack of any sense of worth. John uses this illustration to give us a real insight into God's holiness. It is more than just the absence of sin, it is the very brightness of His presence that gives meaning and direction and visibility to life.

Recently our children were talking about a celebrity who is blind. They remarked what a terrible thing it would be never to know what color is. I'd never thought about it in that way, but color only comes from the presence of light. That which makes objects so attractive, a sunrise, a sunset, the green of the field, the color of the flowers is only visible because of the property of light. God's holiness is not just a neutral quality of perfection. It is a positive quality that the psalmist reflected, "Ascribe to the Lord in the glory of his name; worship the Lord in holy array" (Ps. 29:2).

Based upon this contrast of light and darkness, John also presents two options in regard to fellowship. "If we say we have fellowship with him while we walk in darkness, we lie and do not live according to the truth" (1 John 1:6). To know God and to have fellowship with Him means that we will walk in the beauty of light with direction and understanding. If we are walking in the darkness, stumbling along with no meaning or beauty to life, then we don't have any fellowship with God because the God who is light gives all of those things to life.

It is easy to say we have fellowship. A test of whether we do actually have it or not is how closely we walk with the Father. How can that be measured? John turns the idea around and says, "But if we walk in the light, as he is in the light, we have fellowship with one another, and the blood of Jesus his Son cleanses us from all sin" (1:7). Walking in light produces not only fellowship with God, but also it demands that we have fellowship with His children. Interestingly enough, this is one of the toughest tests. There are many of us who would like to profess our holiness by the fact that we have no fellowship with the people of the world, and particularly with many of the family of God. Yet we know that the sign of communion with God is walking in light. But progressing to fellowship with one another can be a revealing indication of one's spiritual condition.

To further our understanding of God's holiness, let's take a closer look at the grammar in First John, for it is meaningful to us here. The verbs are primarily in the present tense. In Greek grammar, this means that there is continuity of action. Therefore, John is really saying if we *keep on* walking in the light, as He is *always* light, then we *continue* having fellowship with one another.

Also designed into this fellowship with other Christians is the principle of forgiveness. "The blood of Jesus his Son cleanses us from all sin" (1:7). God's holiness touches us and dispels the darkness because the blood of Jesus Christ keeps on cleansing us or forgiving us from all sin. The continuing action of God in our lives not only affects our relationships with others, but it keeps on cleansing our lives.

Based on these two implications, John then presents us with some interesting options. Many of us refuse to face the reality of sin. To us John says, "If we say we have no sin, we deceive ourselves, and the truth is not in us" (1:8). It reminds me of Paul's picture of the man who looks in the mirror and walks away forgetting what manner of man he really is. John is saying that we're kidding ourselves if we say that we do not sin, for the reality of life is that we *do* sin. Any alternative to this truth is untenable. There is, however, an option that is different, because if we are confessing our sin, then God is being faithful and just to forgive us our sin and to continue cleansing us from all unrighteousness (1 John 1:9). The path of fellowship with God and with others is the path of confession and cleansing.

One of the things that always amazes me about many of us who proclaim the Gospel is how often our sermons show how right we are, when in reality much of the time we're way off base. Therefore, we need to confess both to God and to man that we are sinning and find from God His just and faithful promise of forgiveness. Not only must this be done because of the sin that we're aware of, but also for forgiveness of *all* our wrong doing. This is the beautiful holiness of God which withdraws darkness and in addition touches and transforms us with light.

A second option that John presents is that "If we say we have not sinned, we make him a liar, and his word is not in us" (1:10). Notice how the past tense says that all of us have sinned. It proclaims that in the past, sin has not been a part of our life, and we have made of God a liar, and His Word isn't in

70

us. Sin is the ever-present part of humanity within us. God's light removes darkness, and His Son pays the price that there might be forgiveness.

John unites these two options when he says, "My little children, I am writing this to you so that you may not sin; but if any one does sin, we have an advocate with the Father, Jesus Christ the righteous; and he is the expiation for our sins, and not for ours only but also for the sins of the whole world" (2:1–2). Keep in mind that the design of fellowship and forgiveness is not to permit or to promote sin. Rather it is designed to prevent sin. But if any one of us does sin, we have a partnership with the Father, and he will forgive us of our sins. The death of Christ is the Holy One of God taking the penalty for our sins.

As one has portrayed it, these two verses present the courtroom of the heavens. God is the righteous judge, Jesus Christ the defense attorney, the advocate, and Satan the accuser. When I sin, Satan enters into the presence of God and says, "Judge, Your law says the soul that sinneth must die. Phil Hook has sinned; I demand the death penalty." Jesus Christ, the righteous, my advocate, my Paraclete, my defense attorney, says, "Father, I died to pay the price for his sin." And then the judge says, "Case dismissed. Defendant forgiven." You see, God's holiness provides that our walk might be holy, first of all by realizing our sin and further as we confess and find within that confession our forgiveness. We must learn that this whole process keeps us from wanting to do that which is offensive to God and against His character.

The implications found in the holiness and the righteousness of God are easily determined. He is interested in knowing that there is an absence of sin in our life. His hatred for sin is great enough that He hurts very deeply when we begin to do wrong. However, when we do sin, God can accomplish something through our shortcomings, and so as He continues to work in our lives we become more holy because He is holy. That quality of holiness is utterly necessary to approach God, and it is God alone who provides it.

71

STUDY QUESTIONS

1. What does it mean that "God is light and in Him is no darkness at all"? (1 John 1:5). What is light a symbol for? What is darkness a symbol for? Why is light a good synonym for God?

2. If we say we are friends with God and walk with Him, yet our lives are full of sin, what are we doing? Why?

3. If we walk in the light, what two things happen?

4. Is anyone perfect? If we claim we are, who are we kidding? Has anyone except Jesus never done anything wrong?

5. How do we receive God's forgiveness of our sin? How many sins does He forgive us of?

6. What should we do about this today?

8

God Is Truth

One of the most tragic figures in history is a man by the name of Pilate. He happened to be a Roman procurator in the area of Jerusalem at the time of the death of the Lord. The Jews couldn't put Jesus to death without permission from Rome. So they brought Jesus to Pilate with their accusation, "He claims to be King of the Jews." Pilate then confronted Jesus and asked if He was indeed the King of the Jews. Hearing that He was, Pilate asked if this Man thought He was a threat to Rome. "No, if My kingdom were from this world, My men would fight. But My kingdom is not from this world." Pilate announced to the people that he found no wrong in this man who called himself King of the Jews. Once again Pilate asked Jesus if he were King of the Jews, for the people continued their outcry. Jesus answered, "Do you say this of your own accord, or did others say it to you about me?" (John 18:34). Pilate wasn't usually treated that way. He was the judge, the ruler, and not accustomed to asking a question and getting a question back. But you see, Jesus never holds back the truth from anybody, king or peasant, who really desires it, so He stopped to find out if Pilate really wanted to know the truth.

"Pilate answered, 'Am I a Jew? Your own nation and the chief priests have handed you over to me; what have you done?' Jesus answered, 'My kingship is not of this world; if my kingship were of the world, my servants would fight, that I might not be handed over to the Jews; but my kingship is not from the world.' Pilate said to him, 'So you are a king?' Jesus answered, 'You say that I am a king. For this I was born, and for this I have come into the world, to bear witness to the truth. Every one who is of the truth hears my voice' " (John 18:35–37). How would you like to be Pilate right now? Pilate became caught in the middle. He threw up his hands and began to question, "What is truth?" Like many politicians who do not like to make a real decision, he washed his hands of the whole question. He told the Jews to proceed with their plan to kill Jesus.

We struggle quite a lot with what is true because so often we know so little of the truth. During a football game when a certain penalty is called, one side will start cheering and the other will boo. Each saw the same thing, but the penalty was called in favor of only one team. One side says the play was called fairly, but the other side disagrees. The television cameras run it again and again and again, and they end up saying that it is hard to tell just exactly what happened. How something looks from one side of the field can be different from how the same thing looks from the other side of the field. This is the kind of problem we run into when we try to define truth.

What would be a good definition of truth? What does it mean to say that God is truth? Is truth that point at which something doesn't change, at which it is always there? Possibly, but don't you think it goes deeper than that? Have we adequately defined the word? When we're searching for truth, what is it that we're searching for? Truth can be the conformity of fact with understanding. But this definition is inadequate to deal with the larger questions of life where insufficient facts define truth.

Asking the question another way, how do we know what we don't know, or how can we know what we can't know? That is one of the most crucial questions in life. Will the sun come up in the morning? How do you know? It always has, we can know from past experience that some things are true, but this does not guarantee the future. A more perplexing question perhaps is how do you know what is beyond the grave? What is out there beyond death? It is important that we know because if something is out there, it makes a difference about life. In Acts 17, when Paul went to Athens, he started telling them about a God they did not know. Yet they worshiped that very God. They could understand as holy a God who was near them, a God who had created them, but a God who was going to judge did not fit their knowledge. In order to prove this, Paul said, "The times of ignorance God overlooked, but now he commands all men everywhere to repent, because he has fixed a day on which he will judge the world in righteousness by a man whom he has appointed, and of this he has given assurance to all men by raising him from the dead" (Acts 17:30–31).

The Greek mind demanded proof, so the people started arguing whether or not it was possible to have a resurrection from the dead. Was it possible that there was life after death? You see, if Jesus' resurrection proved that there was life after death, then we have a truth that makes a difference about life. That makes a considerable difference in what we do now, because we will be judged after death on the basis of our actions. Some of our world doesn't believe that there is life beyond death. Therefore they believe that it doesn't make any difference what they do. Consequently our philosophy is get all that you can get now, because now is all that you have.

How do they know what they don't really know about life after death? Scripture solves this problem very simply by giving a verifiable event, the Resurrection, that demonstrates the larger truth of judgment and life after death.

You see, at the ultimate level, real truth deals with something beyond what we can know. It deals with the absolute, with something that when it is understood, settles the arguments that we can know.

At the simplest level, we work with truth so that what we think conforms with what is. The larger question about truth is what are the explanations for everything that is? Once again we come to the point of asking, "How do we know what we don't know?"

God Is the True God

"Hear the word which the Lord speaks to you, O house of Israel. Thus says the Lord: 'Learn not the way of the nations, nor be dismayed at the signs of the heavens because the nations are dismayed at them, for the customs of the peoples are false. A tree from the forest is cut down, and worked with an axe by the hands of a craftsman. Men deck it with silver and gold; they fasten it with hammer and nails so that it cannot move. Their idols are like scarecrows in a cucumber field, and they cannot speak; they have to be carried, for they cannot walk. Be not afraid of them, for they cannot do evil, neither is it in them to do good' " (Jer. 10:1–5). You see, for the nations around Israel, God was the boss. The people would make idols out of a tree trunk, cover it with silver and gold, put it up and worship it. But it couldn't talk, nor could it do wrong or even good. It was called a god, but it wasn't a true god, because it couldn't do even the things that people do.

Isaiah and Jeremiah loved to make fun of the gods. They talked about the gods that had to be carried. The God of Israel brought His people up out of Egypt and brought them to safety. The God of Israel carried His people. In contrast, the gods are carried by the people. Jeremiah tried to encourage the people to determine who is their god. He said, "There is none like thee, O Lord; thou art great, and thy name is great in might. Who would not fear thee, O King of the nations? For this is thy due; for among all the wise ones of the nations and in all their kingdoms there is none like thee. They are both stupid and foolish; the instruction of idols is but wood! Beaten silver is brought from Tarshish, and gold from Uphaz. They are the work of the craftsman and of the hands of the goldsmith; their clothing is violet and purple; they are all the work of skilled men. But the Lord is the true God; he is the living God and the everlasting King. At his wrath the earth quakes, and the nations cannot endure his indignation"

(10:6–10). He is saying that among all the gods there is one God who is the true God.

Similarly, in Deuteronomy it is written, "The Rock, his work is perfect; for all his ways are justice. A God of faithfulness and without iniquity, just and right is he" (32:4). The root thought behind the word truth is the word *rock*. Everything is tested by it, even a knife is sharpened against the rock. Something else might be broken by the rock. Moses gives this name to God. The Rock, the one who is the testing point, the measuring point, the faithful one, just and right is He.

The True God Is the Truth

This thought underlies a series of verses in the New Testament that puts together for us how we're to understand truth. The first one is found in the Gospel of John. Jesus has just washed the disciples' feet, and has explained that this is the example for them to follow. They were to wash each other's feet just as He had done. He had served them and in so doing exemplified to them what it means to love. "Little children, yet a little while I am with you. You will seek me; and as I said to the Jews so now I say to you, 'Where I am going you cannot come.' A new commandment I give to you, that you love one another; even as I have loved you, that you also love one another. By this all men will know that you are my disciples, if you have love for one another" (13:33–35). The Lord gives them two great facts. One is that He is leaving and the second is that love is the greatest sign of Christianity. How many of the facts do the disciples hear? They only hear that Jesus is going away and their immediate response isn't "Please help us learn to love one another." Rather they are curious to know where He is going. Jesus says, "Where I am going you cannot follow me now; but you shall follow afterward" (13:36). Peter demands to know why he can't follow the Lord. Jesus tells him that not only will he be disobedient, but also he will deny Christ three times.

Another passage from the New Testament which teaches us that God is truth is found in the fourteenth chapter of John. "Let not your hearts be troubled; believe in God, believe also in me. In my Father's house are many rooms; if it were not so, would I have told you that I go to prepare a place for you? And when I go and prepare a place for you, I will come again and will take you to myself, that where I am you may be also. And you know the way where I am going." Thomas said to him, "Lord, we do not know where you are going; how can we know the way?" And Jesus responds, "I am the way, and the truth, and the life; no one comes to the Father, but by me. If you had known me, you would have known my Father also; henceforth you know him and have seen him" (14:1–7). He is the way to God, He is the truth from God, and He is the life of God. You see, truth in its absolute sense is not a fact, it is a person. Almost any fact we can come up with becomes a point of argument and thus subject to some kind of an exception. But Jesus says that there is one thing for which no exceptions exist and that is Himself. "I am the truth" (John 14:6). He is the measuring point, He is the answer to the question, "How do you know what you don't know?" because He is the source of truth.

The Lord taught His disciples to "Seek first his kingdom and his righteousness, and all these things shall be yours as well" (Matt. 6:33). The world teaches us the opposite viewpoint: "Get all you can while you can." Which is true? Sometimes it looks as if the world is right. If you don't get it now, you never will. But the truth, Jesus says, is that if you reach the right perspectives in the light of His truth, then everything else will fall into its proper perspective as well, because He is the measuring point. He is the focal point of life for the believer.

The True God Who Is the Truth Speaks Truth

Jesus continued to explain in John 16 that He was going away. "I have yet many things to say to you, but you cannot bear them now. When the Spirit of truth comes, he will guide you into all the truth; for he will not speak on his own authority, but whatever he hears he will speak, and he will declare to you the things that are to come. He will glorify me, for he will take what is mine and declare it to you. All that the

Father has is mine; therefore I said that he will take what is mine and declare it to you" (16:12–15). Did you see what the name of this spirit is? He is called the Spirit of Truth who will guide us into truth. He is going to take what Jesus said and taught and thought, and He is going to interpret it to us, so that we, too, can have truth.

The prayer of our Lord in John 17 furthers our understanding of God as truth. After He finished telling the disciples about His departure and about the coming of the Spirit, He then prayed for them. "I have given them thy word; and the world has hated them because they are not of the world, even as I am not of the world. I do not pray that thou shouldst take them out of the world, but that thou shouldst keep them from the evil one. They are not of the world, even as I am not of the world. Sanctify them in the truth; thy word is truth" (17:14–19). Do you see the sequence? God is the test of what is true and He has revealed this to us in Jesus Christ. Also He has given His Spirit, the Spirit of truth, to teach us what that truth is. The last step then is that the Word of God, taught and interpreted by the Spirit of God gives to us the truth of God.

One of the problems with truth as we know it is that it is sometimes subject to contradiction. Consider the dilemma of a man who is walking down the street near his home. He sees a smoldering fire in a neighbor's garage. At the house next door is a hose already hooked up to the faucet. Loving his neighbor means that he will put the fire out. But when he bends over to pick up the hose one of the commandments comes to mind, "Thou shalt not steal." You see, he is caught between the dilemma of doing what is good and taking what is not his. This is the level of human perspective and from that standpoint, sooner or later we make truths contradict. Unless we see truth in the largest picture of what God is saying, we fall short of understanding truth. Out of all the commandments, there are two great statements, "Thou shalt love the Lord thy God with all thy heart, soul, and mind, and also love thy neighbor as thy self." What does the great commandment ask of us? That first of all, we love our neighbor, which means picking up the hose, turning on the water, and putting out the fire. In a similar way, Peter and John, faced with the command to stop preaching, had to say, "We must obey God rather than man" (Acts 5:29).

There is a larger goal of purpose in understanding the truth of God. First of all, the fact that God is truth is the key to *why* we can know. Our search for knowledge has meaning because there is truth. In addition, "God is truth" is the key to why Scripture is to be studied with authority and with reverence—we study because the God who is truth has spoken. Finally, "God is truth" is the key to the proper kind of conduct. As we live our lives in relationship to the truth, then the standards of right and wrong by which we live will conform to the mind of God. The reason that there is such a thing as truth is because there is a God and he has spoken; therefore we not only can *know* truth but we can *live* on the basis of it.

How do we know? We know because God is a person who is truth. How do we know that? Because God has spoken. How do we know what to do? Because God has spoken in truth about what life should be.

STUDY QUESTIONS

1. How is God's truth different from truth as we search for it in the courtroom or in the relationships of life?

2. What is the ultimate measure of what is true and what is not? (Review Pilate's question, "What is truth?")

3. How do we know the truth? (John 14:6 and John 17:17)

4. In the conflicting currents of our world, how do we determine what is truth and what is falsehood? By what standards do we measure truth?

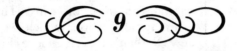

God Is Omniscient

Omniscience—Knowing the Mind

Imagine that you are one of the disciples and a spectator to John the Baptist's teaching in the villages of Israel very early in his ministry. John has started teaching and is ministering to large crowds. Finally, as Jesus goes down to be baptized by John, a dove descends upon Him and a voice sounds from heaven. "The next day Jesus decided to go to Galilee. And he found Philip and said to him, 'Follow me.' Now Philip was from Bethsaida, the city of Andrew and Peter. Philip found Nathanael, and said to him, 'We have found him of whom Moses in the law and also the prophets wrote, Jesus of Nazareth, the son of Joseph. Nathanael said to him, 'Can anything good come out of Nazareth?' Philip said to him, 'Come and see.' " (John 1:43–46).

Understand that Nazareth is sort of a backward town populated by the uneducated and the working class. People from that part of the country could be identified by their dialect. Nathanael, a well educated and highly repected person, hears the people in Nazareth say that they've found the Messiah. Immediately, he would think that the Messiah would come from Jerusalem or Bethlehem.

But Philip says it is Jesus of Nazareth. Jesus of *Nazareth?*

Does that fit? Is that what Moses prophesied? Philip's response is, "Come and see" (1:46).

"Jesus saw Nathanael coming to him, and said of him, 'Behold, an Israelite indeed, in whom is no guile!' Nathanael said to him, 'How do you know me?' Jesus answered him, 'Before Philip called you, when you were under the fig tree, I saw you'" (1:47–48). What are you hearing in that conversation? As a spectator, what do you think of Jesus? Through this conversation, there are some qualities which we can know about God. He knew Nathanael even before Philip called him. Not only did He know him, but He also saw him, and He knew what was inside of him. What are you thinking if you're one of the disciples? Remember that you just met Jesus yesterday. Are you uncomfortable that He can know so much without the benefit of hours and hours of meaningful conversation or time spent together?

Nathanael answers, "Rabbi, you are the Son of God! You are the King of Israel!" (1:49). We can know that Nathanael recognized Jesus' knowledge of all things. Also His observations are penetratingly honest. What kind of a person reaches out and touches your heart in a matter of moments? Because Jesus indicated that Nathanael was a man without guile, Nathanael *knew* He must be the one from God, the Messiah.

Notice Jesus' response. "Because I said to you, I saw you under the fig tree, do you believe? You shall see greater things than these. Truly, truly, I say to you, you will see heaven opened, and the angels of God ascending and descending upon the Son of man" (1:50–51). Not only is there an openness and an honesty, but also there's a prediction, "You *will* see."

Furthermore, there is a promise. Jesus indicates to Nathanael that this is just the beginning. If he has a faith to understand the Christ now, there's no limit to the faith he can have. It works the same way with us.

Parallel to this confrontation between Jesus and Nathanael, we also read in Mark 2 about the Lord's early ministry. Here he has returned to Galilee after being baptized by John. "And when he returned to Capernaum after some days, it was reported that he was at home. And many were gathered together, so that there was no longer room for them, not even about the door; and he was preaching the word to them. And they came, bringing to him a paralytic carried by four men. And when they could not get near him because of the crowd, they removed the roof above him; and when they had made an opening, they let down the pallet on which the paralytic lay" (2:1–4).

Can you imagine what it would be like to be in a meeting while the roofing is being removed? It would have created quite a commotion. Yet interestingly enough, it doesn't seem to disrupt a thing. Finally they carve a hole big enough and get some ropes and let a paralyzed man down where Jesus is teaching. "And when Jesus saw *their* faith, he said to the paralytic, 'My son, your sins are forgiven' " (2:5). How much faith does it take to get healed? It's important to see that we need only faith enough to bring someone to Jesus.

Jesus said to the paralytic that his sins were forgiven. Why, then, do you think he was brought to the gathering? Apparently he was brought to be healed but thus far Jesus hasn't done that. "Now some of the scribes were sitting there, questioning in their hearts, 'Why does this man speak thus? It is blasphemy! Who can forgive sins but God alone?' And immediately Jesus, perceiving in his spirit that they thus questioned within themselves, said to them, 'Why do you question thus in your hearts? Which is easier, to say to the paralytic, "Your sins are forgiven," or to say "Rise, take up your pallet and walk"? But that you may know that the Son of man has authority on earth to forgive sins'—he said to the paralytic—'I say to you, rise, take up your pallet and go home' " (2:6–11). Now what happens to the paralytic? He is healed immediately in both his body and soul. "And he arose, and immediately took up the pallet and went out before them all; so that they were all amazed and glorified God, saying, 'We never saw anything like this!' " (2:12).

The event must have been disconcerting to His audience in several ways. First, the miracle was unexplainable from their perspective. Second, it was related to the power to forgive sins. Third, Jesus seemingly had "read their minds" and with an incredible confirmation. It must have been disturbing to be around Jesus and have your mind read and your doubts confronted.

Omniscience—Knowing the Future

Our word omniscience comes from the Greek "skio" which means knowledge and the word "Omni" which means all or every: all knowing. God's omniscience is particularly evident during various stages of Jesus' ministry. Imagine that you are with the disciples at the end of Jesus' ministry and are with them in the upper room. Jesus has shared with His disciples in the Passover. He has told them that there is a responsibility in spite of the fact that God is at work. "For the Son of man goes as it has been determined; but woe to that man by whom he is betrayed!" (Luke 22:22).

What is He saying? Was Jesus surprised that He would soon die? He's the lamb slain before the foundations of the world. Therefore He says that what is going to happen is exactly what has been planned. In spite of Jesus' warning that He would die, the disciples still panicked. He also told them that Judas' betrayal would be wrong and that he would bear responsibility for his own deceitfulness.

For our peace of mind, we like to make it one way or the other. We like to think that our lives are all planned and therefore we don't have to do anything about it. That's the Calvinist. What will be will be. God planned it all and we just have to sit here and check off His elective work. The other side, the Arminian, likes to say that events in our lives won't happen unless we cause them to happen. So, they say, we need to work at saving ourselves. Jesus puts both sides together in one sentence when He says what God has planned is going to happen and Judas is responsible for the betrayal. This statement by Jesus is one of the most profound theological statements in the Gospels, but the disciples really don't pay any attention to it. When they hear that He is to be betrayed, they ask, "Is it I?" But they recover from that very question and pass on to the question that is more important to them.

They suffer from a chronic desire for greatness and in so doing, move from a tremendous theological statement to the simplest of selfish arguments, "Which one of us is the greatest?"

Jesus answers them, "Simon, Simon, behold, Satan demanded to have you, that he might sift you like wheat, but I have prayed for you that your faith may not fail; and when you have turned again, strengthen your brethren" (22:31–32). Peter, not understanding the depth of the message, says that he understands and he's ready to go to prison with Jesus or even die for him. Look, though, at what Jesus has just said. What does He already know? He knows that He will be betrayed and that Peter will be the one to deny Him. He also knows that Peter will return to strengthen the brethren. This is one of the most encouraging sentences in all of Scripture because who of us hasn't occasionally been a Peter? That wasn't the end for him, though. In Christ, he could find hope beyond denial. In fact, out of denial is going to come strength.

What else does Jesus know? He told Peter that out of the denial he would be stronger and better than he had ever been. Jesus also knew that Satan would be at the root of the failure. Does this remind you of Job, when Satan came before God and said, "I'd like You, too, if I were Job." Can you hear the conversation about Peter? "Sure, Lord. No wonder he follows You. Look how good You are to him." Satan persists, "You take care of him; You feed him; You make him a hero all the time. He was nothing but a bum fisherman." And the reply is, "Come with Me a little while and I'll show you what he's made of."

Jesus also said, "I have prayed for you that your faith may not fail" (22:32). If you had checked with Peter a few hours later, what would you have said about his faith? It looked as if his faith had failed. In reality, however, it had only wavered. Remember, though, who had been doing the praying. Did Peter pray, "Lord, I denied You once and now I've got to stop." No, Peter didn't even know the denial was taking place. Do you find that a little bit encouraging? How many of us neglect to pray when we ought to be praying the most?

Fortunately, Jesus knows and He prays on our behalf constantly. When we come to Romans 8, we find out that in addition to Jesus, even the Holy Spirit murmurs on our behalf. And from that we can derive tremendous comfort.

Similarly, Jesus' knowledge is also comforting. How would it be to walk along beside Him and realize that He already knew what you were thinking before you said it out loud? Or how would it feel to know that He knew the very depths of your heart and could tell you what would happen before it occurred, or even what Satan would do in your life? What would be your reaction to hear Him say, "I know these things, and I'm praying for you, and it will turn out O.K., so don't worry." That is disconcerting, only because we like to protect our innermost thoughts from being known by anyone else. The fact that God already knows those thoughts is reassuring as well.

Omniscience—Knowing What Might Have Been

We can get another idea of God's omniscience from Matthew 11. At this point, we are about two years into His ministry. The Lord has done an enormous amount of preaching and healing, and people are being forced to make decisions. Chapters 11 and 12 record a pattern of rejection that develops among the nations. As this trend continues, Jesus "began to upbraid the cities where most of his mighty works had been done, because they did not repent. 'Woe to you, Chorazin! woe to you, Bethsaida! for if the mighty works done in you had been done in Tyre and Sidon, they would have repented long ago in sackcloth and ashes. But I tell you, it shall be more tolerable on the day of judgment for Tyre and Sidon than for you. And you, Capernaum, will you be exalted to heaven? You shall be brought down to Hades. For if the mighty works done in you had been done in Sodom, it would have remained until this day. But I tell you that it shall be more tolerable on the day of judgment for the land of Sodom than for you'" (11:20–24). What do you hear Him saying? He knows what will happen on the Judgment Day, therefore, He knows something of the future. More than that, He not only knew what did happen, but also what could have happened. He knows the future, He knows the past, and He knows what might have been as well as what will be.

Now we're beginning to get down to the depths of what God's knowledge really is. Have you ever wondered what it would be like if you had been born a different person? Probably every one of us has pondered that question from time to time. What if I had been richer, poorer, better looking, a better athlete? Do you ever play the "what if" game? There are some answers to those questions. Let's look at one of them by remembering the story of Sodom. How many people would God have been willing to save Sodom for? Lot lived there with his two children and his wife, who disobeyed and looked back. Who did God send to Sodom to witness? He sent angels, Abraham, and particularly Lot who "vexed his righteous soul over what was happening in his city." But nobody believed him, nor did he do much about the disbelief. Why do you think God sent Lot and not Jesus to Sodom? Perhaps that is an unanswerable question, but in part we can suggest that it wasn't within God's time plan for Jesus to go at that time. Were the people in Sodom innocent? Were they responsible? Was it unfair that they had judgment rained on them? But God *knew* that if Jesus had gone, it would have been different.

Do you see the knowledge of God? Have you ever thought that had you been a disciple you would have been any different than Jesus' companions? Would you have denied Jesus? Or betrayed him? Usually we think that we wouldn't do such a thing. But when we honestly take a look at what we do, we're more like the disciples than we realize. Out of the myriad of options, God didn't send Jesus to Sodom, nor was He sent to Tyre and Sidon. But God knows what would have happened if Jesus had been sent to another place at another time. You see, judgment for Sodom was tough. But judgment someday is going to be according to the knowledge of God. God understands, and He knows the options. Can you imagine being God when a farmer is praying for rain at the same time a mother is praying for dry weather for her daughter's outdoor wedding reception? Multiply that situation by about a billion people and be glad that God is God with His infinite knowledge to deal with our prayers and needs.

The infinite quality of God's knowledge far exceeds anything that we dream about. Because His knowledge of each of us is so great, there are no mistakes. On one hand that's disturbing because it seems to cut down on our freedom, but on the other hand, that is comforting because the Lord says that judgment will be in light of what was and what might have been. God knows our deepest longings. He sees in us the light of the strongest hidden desires of our hearts and acts accordingly for our benefit. The God who searches the hearts of man understands us even before we build walls around ourselves to hide our true natures.

Omniscience—Knowing Me

A good picture of the God who not only knows what might have been but also who knows us totally is seen in Psalm 139. When you begin seeing how great God's knowledge really is, as well as seeing the potentiality of that knowledge, it can be bothersome and comforting at the same time. But in this Psalm, David brings that knowledge down to one of the most comforting things in life. "Lord, thou hast searched me and known me! Thou knowest when I sit down and when I rise up" (139:1–2). Think about sitting down and standing up. Are we ever aware of those actions? Are we ever conscious of the mechanics of balancing one foot in front of the other so we don't fall when we stand up? God is concerned with that.

God is also concerned that we are known in the deepest corners of our heart and soul. How many people can you claim to know who have really searched out knowing you? It can be a valuable experience. You're fortunate if there is one person who knows you and extremely fortunate if two or three people have decided to take the time to know you well and affirm you as a person.

Probably the saddest day that I shared with many freshmen students in college was several weeks after the beginning of their year in school. Those kids would stop by the office and they'd say, "You know, I thought that when I came to college, I'd get a roommate who would be interested in the same things I was, who would want to become good friends. But now, I've been here and my roommate has other interests and we never spend time together, or with other kids in the dorm." That dream of having a close friend, somebody who really cared about them, was shattered. Sadly enough, most of us have learned to live without such a close friend. But the psalmist says that things can be different if only we would realize God's all-knowing spirit. "Thou discernest my thoughts from afar" (139:2). You see, God searches out His knowledge of us and even when we're a long way off, He knows what is happening. He knows what we're thinking. "Thou searchest out my path and my lying down, and are acquainted with all my ways" (139:3). Does anybody know you that well? To me the comforting and incredible thing is that God does, and He still loves us.

"Even before a word is on my tongue, lo, O Lord, thou knowest it altogether" (139:4). Where are the words before we speak them? They're in our minds, right? When does the Lord know them? Fortunately, most of the time, we don't say everything that comes into our minds. But God knows all of those thoughts. Fascinating, isn't it? How many of us want to be known so well that our thoughts are known? I used to tell students that I was going to invent a system whereby they could see their thoughts on a screen by hooking up a helmet to a TV set. How many volunteers do you think I would get to put it on? Not only does *God* know those thoughts, but also He knows them completely.

An interesting parallel to this Psalm is found in Matthew 6. "And when you pray, you must not be like the hypocrites; for they love to stand and pray in the synagogues and at the street corners, that they may be seen by men. Truly, I say to you, they have their reward. But when you pray, go into your room and shut the door and pray to your Father who is in secret; and your Father who sees in secret will reward you" (6:5–6). This isn't all the Scriptures teach about prayer, but Jesus here is countering the standard kind of prayer of that day, a one-sided connection which was not talking to God. Rather, it was talking to God so that men could see you, and think you were religious for all the time you spent in conversation with God. "And in praying do not heap up empty phrases as the Gentiles do; for they think that they will be heard for their many words" (6:7). Do you ever get the feeling that some people pray to see how long they can communicate with the Father? "Do not be like them, for your Father knows what you need before you ask him" (6:8). Sometimes in our limited understanding of God, we aren't too sure that He knows all the things we think He needs to know. Our prayers are full of information in order to help God make good decisions about our lives.

If God already knows our thoughts before we say them and if He already knows our needs before we ask them, then why is it necessary to even pray? One could say that we're commanded to pray. Also, prayer can be for our own benefit. When prayers are answered, we know our faith in God is strengthened and confirmed. Sometimes even hearing ourselves converse with God is good for us. But a purpose of fellowship and dependence seems to precede all the other reasons. I began to understand this when our children were little. The only words they knew, we had taught them. Yet we loved to hear them say the words even though we knew before they spoke what they would say. It was our delight to listen to their needs and act on their behalf.

Many times we miss the essence of communicating with God in prayer. It isn't educating God and it isn't trying to get God to do something He wouldn't ordinarily do. You see, God is already committed to loving us. The beautiful thing about God is that He listens without interjecting several suggestions and comments before we're through talking. Then when we become quiet and listen, we are able to hear God speaking to us.

Let's take a look at Psalm 77 to see an example of what God listens to. "I cry aloud to God, aloud to God, that he may hear me. In the day of my trouble I seek the Lord; in the night my hand is stretched out without wearying; my soul refuses to be comforted. I think of God, and I moan; I meditate, and my spirit faints. Thou dost hold my eyelids from closing; I am so troubled that I cannot speak. I consider the days of old, I remember the years long ago. I commune with my heart in the night; I meditate and search my spirit: 'Will the Lord spurn forever, and never again be favorable? Has his steadfast love forever ceased? Are his promises at an end for all time? Has God forgotten to be gracious? Has he in anger shut up his compassion?' "(77:1–9). Have you ever talked to God like that? Can you imagine God having to listen to such complaints and then asking David to write it down so others could benefit from those thoughts? Somehow or other, God would rather have us say what is troubling us than to be quiet and not talk to Him at all.

After encouraging us to pray, He teaches us the simplest kind of prayer, "Our Father who art in heaven, Hallowed be thy name." Lord, what I really want in this world is what You want, "Thy kingdom come." Lord, I really don't want to change Your will. "Thy will be done." Lord, I know that we'll eat in a little while, but give me this day what I need for life. "Give us this day our daily bread; and forgive us our debts, as we also have forgiven our debtors; and lead us not into temptation, but deliver us from evil" (Matt. 6:9–13). Lord, please don't leave us tempted out in the desert to be put to the test by the evil one. Is God going to do these things? Is His will going to be done? Do you see what He is saying? "Lord, even before the thought in my mind becomes words, you know them altogether." You see, God's knowledge of us is so great that there are no surprises, yet He loves us. He cares about us and invites us to talk about what happens to us.

Remember David's words in Psalm 139? "Thou dost beset me behind and before, and layest thy hand upon me. Such knowledge is too wonderful for me; it is high, I cannot attain it" (139:5–6). A few years ago I was at the Dallas airport to catch a plane to Los Angeles. The elderly lady seated next to me was obviously very uncomfortable with concern over the flight. When we took off, I asked if she wanted to hold my hand so she wouldn't be frightened. She did then and also when we landed. Somehow or other a hand made all the difference in the world, even a stranger's hand—the touch of someone in the time of struggle. This is what the psalmist is saying—that God not only knows us totally and perfectly, but also He puts His hand upon us, precedes us, and follows us so that we have no need to be afraid.

Do you see the knowledge of God? It is an awesome thing, but God's knowledge doesn't stay off in the distance somewhere. It comes right down to where He knows us completely. That understanding comforts us, and it goes back to praying. Many times we want to pray and haven't the slightest idea what to say, but God already knows what we're thinking. We can say that we lay before Him all that we are, and trust Him to listen and hear, believing that God will never misuse knowing His children totally.

STUDY QUESTIONS

1. Explain what Jesus knew about people and how He knew it. (Look at John 1:47–49, Matthew 10:29–31, Mark 2:6–8.)

2. God's knowledge includes everything, even what might have happened. He knows the answers to the questions that begin with "what if . . . ?" Look up Matthew 11:23–24. If Jesus instead of Lot had gone to Sodom, what would have happened? What difference will it make someday in the judgment? Why?

3. In Psalm 139, David tells us how well God knows us. Make a list using verses 1 through 5 and explain what God knows about you.

4. If God knows us so well how should this affect our conduct? Our thoughts? Our understanding of ourselves when God knows everything about us and He still loves us?

10

God Is Omnipresent

Have you ever been amazed that God can be with you and at the same time with your friends and relatives in distant cities? This is the characteristic of God which we call omnipresence. Because of this, God can be and is everywhere present in His universe.

Omnipresence—God Always Present in Time and Space

An indication of this characteristic of God is found in Matthew 28:16–20. "Now the eleven disciples went to Galilee, to the mountain to which Jesus had directed them. And when they saw him they worshiped him; but some doubted. And Jesus came and said to them, 'All authority in heaven and on earth has been given to me. Go therefore and make disciples of all nations, baptizing them in the name of the Father and of the Son and of the Holy Spirit, teaching them to observe all that I have commanded you; and lo, I am with you always, to the close of the age.'"

Notice that Jesus quite clearly says, "I am with you *always.*" I think the key to this sentence began several weeks earlier in the life of the Lord, when at the end of John 13, He told his disciples that where He was going, they couldn't go with Him. The disciples panicked, "Where are You going? Why can't we come? Where are you going? We don't know

93

the way." We must realize that on that side of the cross, there was no effective way to answer their questions, because they didn't understand what was to come as Jesus understood it. They had no conception of His death and resurrection. They couldn't comprehend the idea of a new body and a different way of relating to Jesus. The Lord gave the disciples a job to fulfill, and along with it a promise that He would be with them even to the end of the age.

The fascinating thing is that Jesus didn't just say He would be with them as they fulfilled His commands, He also said He'd be with them everywhere they went. You see, God's omnipresence is His presence not only in space, but also in time. An example of God's omnipresence is found in one of the Old Testament books. The prophet Jeremiah warned the nation of coming judgment and that there could be no turning back. In this particular instance He spoke of all the false prophets who felt that they had nothing to worry about because the final days weren't really that near.

"Concerning the prophets: My heart is broken within me, all my bones shake; I am like a drunken man, like a man overcome by wine, because of the Lord and because of his holy words. For the land is full of adulterers; because of the curse the land mourns, and the pastures of the wilderness are dried up. Their course is evil, and their might is not right. Both the prophet and priest are ungodly; even in my house I have found their wickedness, says the Lord" (23:9–11). Such unfortunate circumstances are exposed and Jeremiah continues to tell of the evils of the land.

He then begins to warn of the prophets' false messages. "Thus says the Lord of hosts: 'Do not listen to the words of the prophets who prophesy to you, filling you with vain hopes; they speak visions of their own minds, not from the mouth of the Lord. They say continually to those who despise the word of the Lord, "It shall be well with you"; and to every one who stubbornly follows his own heart, they say, "No evil shall come upon you" ' " (23:16–17). You see, the prophets are going against the basis of what God's nature is, and the example He sets in His message. The people who are being disobedient are saying not to worry about their failure to obey. When judgment is now for Jeremiah just a few years away, and before that time when he enters captivity, the people continue to exclaim that God wouldn't return so soon.

"For who among them has stood in the council of the Lord to perceive and to hear his word, or who has given heed to his word and listened? Behold, the storm of the Lord! Wrath has gone forth, a whirling tempest; it will burst upon the head of the wicked. The anger of the Lord will not turn back until he has executed and accomplished the intents of his mind. In the latter days you will understand it clearly" (23:18–20). Even in those days, they had trouble understanding the tension between the false prophets and the true Lord. Jeremiah continues, "I did not send the prophets, yet they ran; I did not speak to them, yet they prophesied. But if they had stood in my council, then they would have proclaimed my words to my people, and they would have turned them from their evil way, and from the evil of their doings"(23:21–22).

The Lord follows these verses with "Am I a God at hand, says the Lord, and not a God afar off? Can a man hide himself in secret places so that I cannot see him? Do I not fill heaven and earth? says the Lord" (23:23–24). The prophets are wondering if they will be faced with a whirling tempest. But God responds to them, "Where are you going to hide? Is there anywhere you can go that I won't see you? Is there anywhere you can be that I'm not there?"

Omnipresence–God Is Greater Than Time or Space

With this as a background, let's look at another interesting insight into this characteristic of God. Remember in Second Samuel that David sat in his palace one day and looked out at the tent of Israel and he said, "How is it that I live in a palace and God still lives in the tent?" He called Nathan the prophet and said that he would build a house for the Lord. And Nathan said, "That's a great idea, go ahead." When Nathan went back to his room to pray, God said, "Tell David that he can prepare for the temple, but that he can't build it." However, God did allow David's son, Solomon, to build the temple. So great and magnificent was the structure that it became one of the seven wonders of the world about 1000 B.C.

In First Kings we read the dedicatory prayer for the temple. "Solomon stood before the altar of the Lord in the presence of all the assembly of Israel, and spread forth his hands toward heaven; and said, 'O Lord, God of Israel, there is no God like thee, in heaven above or on earth beneath, keeping covenant and showing steadfast love to thy servants who walk before thee with all their heart; who hast kept with thy servant David my father what thou didst declare to him; yea, thou didst speak with thy mouth, and with thy hand hast fulfilled it this day. Now therefore, O Lord, God of Israel, keep with thy servant David my father what thou hast promised him, saying, "There shall never fail you a man before me to sit upon the throne of Israel, if only your sons take heed to their way, to walk before me as you have walked before me." Now therefore, O God of Israel, let thy word be confirmed, which thou hast spoken to thy servant David my father. But will God indeed dwell on the earth? Behold, heaven and the highest heaven cannot contain thee; how much less this house which I have built! Yet have regard to the prayer of thy servant and to his supplication, O Lord my God, hearkening to the cry and to the prayer which thy servant prays before thee this day; that thy eyes may be open night and day toward this house, the place of which thou hast said, "My name shall be there," that thou mayest hearken to the prayer which thy servant offers toward this place. And hearken thou to the supplication of thy servant and of thy people Israel, when they pray toward this place; yea, hear thou in heaven thy dwelling place; and when thou hearest, forgive' " (8:22–30).

Here is another step towards gaining insight into the presence of God. Solomon starts with the magnificence of His greatness. Heaven and all of the universe is not large enough to contain the Lord, but now He is choosing to live in the temple. One of the mysteries of the nature of God is that He is literally everywhere, yet He is right with us all the time. Where two or three are gathered in His name, He is there in the midst of them. How many places do you think there are on a Sunday morning where two or three are gathered in His name? The great size of God we call immensity—He is everywhere present in the universe.

Omnipresence—God's Presence Whether Recognized or Not

Solomon's prayer puzzles over how this can be. How can God be everywhere and yet present with us? How can He be so great and yet choose to dwell among His people? Perhaps some of these questions can be answered in the Book of Acts. God is in the near and also in the far. He's everywhere, yet localized. On the way to Athens to address the people from Mars Hill, Paul noticed many evidences of idols and perceived that the Athenians were very religious people. But he also noticed one shrine designed to worship an unknown god. "What therefore you worship as unknown, this I proclaim to you. The God who made the world and everything in it, being Lord of heaven and earth, does not live in shrines made by man, nor is he served by human hands, as though he needed anything, since he himself gives to all men life and breath and everything. And he made from one every nation of men to live on all the face of the earth, having determined allotted periods and the boundaries of their habitation, that they should seek God, in the hope that they might feel after him and find him. Yet he is not far from each one of us, for 'In him we live and move and have our being' " (17:23–28).

Does this add another dimension to our understanding of God? The disciples are aware of Jesus, Jeremiah is aware of what God is like, and Solomon talks about the majesty of God. But Paul says to the Athenians that God is near whether you like it or not. You worship what you think are the gods, but the real God, the Creator, is also the present God. He is always nearer to you than you think. The ultimate proof of this God is the Resurrection, the guarantee of judgment—and that is as far as the Greek people want to go. It is nice for them to talk about the God who is here, but when He is also a God who acts, and a God who intervenes in time and who knows and guarantees that there is a judgment day ahead, it breaks the meaning of their faith. Understand that He is a God who is here—*always* here, whether we know it or not.

Omnipresence—Where Can I Go?

Psalm 139 sheds more light on God's omnipresence. After the psalmist ponders how totally he is known by God, he broadens this knowledge by asking, "Whither shall I go from thy Spirit? Or whither shall I flee from thy presence?" (139:7). Few people think of themselves as going anywhere other than heaven after death, but everyone is afraid of the process of getting there. Even in the loneliest moment that we can perceive, God is there. The Christian has a promise that death is a victory. One of the most beautiful pictures of death is in Luke 16 with the rich man and Lazarus. After Lazarus dies, it is written that the angels carried him to Abraham's bosom. The real pallbearers of the universe are the angels. The real companion of death is God.

Where shall I flee? Where shall I go? Heaven? That's Your home. Even in death You are with me, "If I take the wings of the morning and dwell in the uttermost parts of the sea, even there thy hand shall lead me, and thy right hand shall hold me" (139:9–10). In similar circumstances, let's remember Jonah. God told him to go and preach to the Ninevites, but Jonah was hesitant to do so. Unless someone preached to them, they would be judged, but Jonah thought they didn't deserve to hear the gospel. In fleeing from this command, Jonah goes away to the right town, to the right boat, to the right storm, to the right fish, to the right beach, and thus on his way to Nineveh.

Is it possible that sometimes we want to escape God's presence? Are we happily carnal Christians? That concept in itself is not so accurate, but haven't you ever been tempted to take a couple of weeks off and not think about your faith or anything involved with it? There's no such thing. Even through the rebellion and the carnality of Jonah's life, God went right along with him. There are no mistakes made in Jonah's voyage and in each step of the way, he comes face to face with God again.

The psalmist continues, "If I say, 'Let only darkness cover me, and the light about me be night,' even the darkness is not dark to thee, the night is as bright as the day; for darkness is as light with thee" (139:11–12). Man is very much like the ostrich. He buries his head, and because he can't see, he thinks he can't be seen. We approach night time in a similar way. We do all kinds of things at night that we wouldn't do in the daytime, because we think we can't be seen. But look at what the psalmist says about God. Darkness is not dark to God, in fact the darkness is as the light to Him. God is not caught in the world of light and dark, or even shades of gray. He sees it all the same.

One of my college roommates used to let me borrow his car in the evenings. Every time I left he would say to me, "Remember one thing. God can see in the dark as well as He can see in the light." I knew that, but somehow or other, I always hated to hear him say it. I had no intentions of doing anything wrong, but I had a few hopes that something might come up. It is sort of the "by chance" syndrome of behavior. You see, though, that's fallible because there's no darkness to God.

God's omnipresence is brought to a more distinct relationship to ourselves in First Corinthians 6. "All things are lawful for me, but not all things are helpful. All things are lawful for me, but I will not be enslaved by anything" (6:12). "Do you not know that your bodies are members of Christ? Shall I therefore take the members of Christ and make them members of a prostitute? Never! Do you not know that he who joins himself to a prostitute becomes one body with her? For as it is written, 'The two shall become one flesh.' But he who is united to the Lord becomes one spirit with him. Shun immorality. Every other sin which a man commits is outside the body; but the immoral man sins against his own body. Do you not know that your body is a temple of the Holy Spirit within you, which you have from God? You are not your own; you were bought with a price. So glorify God in your body" (6:15–20).

In these few lines is found the explanation of the promise, "Lo, I am with you always even to the end of the age." The first step in understanding God's presence is that we who are believers become one with Christ. We are in fact a part of His body, a member of His church. Consequently, our bodies become the dwelling place, the temple of the Holy Spirit within us—the gift of God. And that transforms our bodies from being just another combination of flesh and blood, a complex energy system that we call mankind, into a very localized dwelling place of the presence of God.

"Do not be mismated with unbelievers. For what partnership have righteousness and iniquity? Or what fellowship has light with darkness? What accord has Christ with Belial? Or what has a believer in common with an unbeliever? What agreement has the temple of God with idols? For we are the temple of the living God; as God said, 'I will live in them and move among them, and I will be their God, and they shall be my people. Therefore come out from them, and be separate from them, says the Lord, and touch nothing unclean; then I will welcome you, and I will be a father to you, and you shall be my sons and daughters, says the Lord Almighty.' Since we have these promises, beloved, let us cleanse ourselves from every defilement of body and spirit, and make holiness perfect in the fear of God" (2 Cor. 6:14–7:1). These two passages from First and Second Corinthians are the counterpart to Solomon's prayer. Solomon asks, "How is it, Lord, that You whom heaven and earth cannot contain, You who are everywhere present in the universe, will make Your home with us in this building that I have built?" But the new covenant miracle is a greater miracle than that. His presence is not within a building. His presence is in a body. This old body tied to all of the problems and all of the things of this world becomes the dwelling place of the presence of God. Reach out and touch some believer near to you. You've touched the dwelling place of God. Striking, isn't it? God is no farther away than someone in whose body He lives. There is another implication to God's presence. If this is the dwelling place of God, if God is present within me, then it makes a difference what I do with my body. It makes a difference to whom I couple my body sexually and it makes a difference how I use my body and where I take my body.

In the same way that we realize we are the dwelling place of an omnipresent God, we must also realize how to worship that

God. Some people are honestly aware of what worship really is. In some churches there is an atmosphere of awe and reverence. Not only are the worshipers conscious that God is present, but also that He is present in their bodies. They understand what being in the presence of God really means. Worship is the name for that response—the awe of the presence of God. It would be a mistake to turn a building into something worshipful if we didn't realize the greater worship of the God within us and the temple that we live in. Wherever we go, He not only is there, He's also inside of us at the same time. As long as we live, He's not only always present, but He's always inside. "Do you not know that your body is a temple of the Holy Spirit within you, which you have from God?" (1 Cor. 6:19). Therefore, glorify God, manifest what He is like in your body. It's easy to make light of our bodies, how tall or short, how large or small they are. But if we miss the most cardinal truth that our bodies are a dwelling place for God, we're really missing the beauty of what God has done to us, because He has not changed the outside. He has, though, cleansed and come to dwell on the inside. Therefore, the way we live on the outside should reflect this most wonderful aspect of God—that he is everywhere present with us and within us.

STUDY QUESTIONS

1. Read Acts 17:22–31 about Paul introducing people to their "unknown god." What does this "god" do? Who is he? What should man do?

2. Read Psalm 139. Where does David find God?

3. What should this mean to us when we're frightened? When things seem uncertain? When we are alone?

4. How does this shape your understanding of prayer?

God Is Omnipotent

The last of the omni-attributes gives us another overwhelming insight into the character of God. He not only knows the real as well as the possible and is always present wherever and whenever we need Him, but He is also able to do something about it. God is more than a force. He is an all-powerful person who knows, who is there, and who is able to deliver.

Omnipotence—All Things Are Possible

This characteristic can be seen through Jesus' ministry with His disciples. In Mark 8, Jesus had brought His disciples to a point of faith. He began to teach them what it meant for Him to be the Christ, the Son of the living God, to deny self, and to take up the cross and follow Him. Then He promised that before they died, some of them would see a manifestation of the kingdom and the power of God. Taking three of them up to the top of the mountain, He gave them that vision. He then was transfigured before them, but none of the disciples were to say anything about Jesus' promise. Can you imagine how hard it would be to contain your own excitement at seeing the Christ?

While Jesus was on the mountain with three of the disciples, a man bringing his son to be healed came up to the remaining nine disciples. Notice what happens among them when the man brings his son before them. All at once they are excited about the promise, aggravated because they can't tell anybody, and now they're faced with exercising their own faith in trying to heal the boy. They've witnessed this scene dozens of times. Possibly there was even an argument about which one of them would perform the healing. As they tried to help, the boy became less able to control himself and was showing no signs of being healed. As I picture this scene, about the fifth or sixth time that happened, the scribes and Pharisees began to doubt that the disciples had been taught by Jesus at all. They even think that Jesus must be a fake, or He would be here, too, so where is He? Under this close scrutiny, the last three might say, "In the name of Jesus, I hope it will work."

When Jesus and the three return from the mountain, the scribes almost had the onlookers convinced that the disciples and Jesus, too, were all fakes. "And when they came to the disciples, they saw a great crowd about them, and scribes arguing with them. And immediately all the crowd, when they saw him, were greatly amazed, and ran up to him and greeted him. And he asked them, 'What are you discussing with them?' And one of the crowd answered him, 'Teacher, I brought my son to you, for he has a dumb spirit; and whenever it seizes him, it dashes him down; and he foams and grinds his teeth and becomes rigid; and I asked your disciples to cast it out, and they were not able' " (Mark 9:14–18). They were not able because their trust was in their own power, not the power that God has to heal the sick.

Jesus answers the man in a seldom-seen attitude of impatience. " 'O faithless generation, how long am I to be with you? Bring him to me.' And they brought the boy to him; and when the spirit saw him, immediately it convulsed the boy, and he fell on the ground and rolled about, foaming at the mouth. And Jesus asked his father, 'How long has he had this?' " (9:19–21).

Can you visualize this scene with me? The boy is convulsing and the father is desperate. The disciples no longer try to heal, and probably blend into the background. Amid the confusion, Jesus wants to have a conversation.

"How long has the boy been sick?" Why do you suppose Jesus asked that question? Rebuking the father for not bringing the boy sooner could be the reason. In a different way, though, perhaps He wanted to make a visible demonstration of His power to the scribes, who think that if He really is the Christ and really is all powerful, then He would have arrived sooner. Let us watch what Jesus is going to prove to them. The father answers Jesus, "From childhood. And it has often cast him into the fire and into the water, to destroy him; but if you can do anything, have pity on us and help us" (9:21–22).

Do you understand what could be happening inside the father? How would you like to bring your son before the crowds and be a nine-time loser on getting him healed? How would it be to display your child in that way? Can you hear the desperation in his voice? For the scribes and Pharisees this is a fun game of debate, and for the disciples, it is a tremendous blow to their egos. But for the father, it is sheer desperation. What would the father have settled for at this point? Most probably he would have accepted almost anything—even a slight improvement in his son's condition. His experience taught him that there's no hope, so he only says, "If you can do anything, please help."

Jesus said to him, "If you can! All things are possible to him who believes" (9:23). Do you believe that all things are possible with God? Often we fall into the habit of answering that question beginning with that tiny word, "if." But, you see, there's no "if" to it. All things are possible with God. I doubt, though, that the father understood that. In all honesty the man answers, "I believe; help my unbelief!" The man is right where we are. All things are possible with God, true or false? True, but when we face a problem, do we still answer the same way? The man did something that we usually don't do. He brought both his faith and his doubts before God. What do we normally do? Do we take our doubts to the philosophy professors and put our faith on a back burner? Do we doubt our faith and believe our doubts? Then what happens? The statement says that all things are possible to him who believes. Could it be that the biggest reason we don't pray about a lot of things is that we don't believe God can do anything about them? Faith and doubt walk the same street. We need to bring both to the Lord. One He will reward and the other He will cure.

Let's look at another passage. In Mark 10, Jesus was beginning a journey, "And as he was setting out on his journey, a man ran up and knelt before him, and asked him, 'Good Teacher, what must I do to inherit eternal life?' " (10:17). But when Jesus answered him, "he went away sorrowful; for he had great possessions" (10:22). What kind of man is this? Our first picture of him is running up and kneeling before Jesus, indicating that he is sincere. Rich men usually don't humble themselves in this way. For such a reason, we know that his heart is searching for an honest answer to his question. "And he said to him, 'Teacher, all these I have observed from my youth.' And Jesus looking upon him loved him" (10:20–21). He has the question and Jesus has the response—love. Jesus said to him, "You lack one thing; go, sell what you have, and give to the poor, and you will have treasure in heaven; and come, follow me" (10:21). The commandment that is being broken is the first one—we should have no other gods before us. Where did the man fail? He had kept all the rest of the commandments, yet he worshiped the god of money. He asked the wrong question and he had the wrong god. Those two things were standing between him and eternal life. It was the abundance of his possessions that kept him from following God. Who is Lord in his life? Most surely we know that it is his possessions.

But if you put yourself in the shoes of the disciples for a moment, what do you think you're getting out of following Jesus? You're following the King, and probably you're doing it in order to be somebody. If you're Secretary of the Interior; or Chancellor of the Exchequer; or Secretary of Health, Education and Welfare; what benefits do you think are going to come along with the title? Prestige, power, riches? And we're supposed to give all that money to the poor when there are so many things that can be done with it right here? Look at what Jesus tells the disciples about wealth. " 'How hard it will be for those who have riches to enter the kingdom of God!' And the disciples were amazed at his words" (10:23–24). The disciples knew wealthy people, and they understood this as an indication that Jesus had blessed them materially. Their whole world of understanding is tipped upside down. Those men had a lot of faith; it was just in the wrong place and therefore they are called the "faithless generation."

To the disciples' amazement and shock, "Jesus said to them again, 'Children, how hard it is to enter the kingdom of God! It is easier for a camel to go through the eye of a needle than for a rich man to enter the kingdom of God.' And they were exceedingly astonished, and said to him, 'Then who can be saved?' " (10:24–25). If we only consider riches here, we're missing the point. Had he entered a football locker room, I think he would have preached on how hard it is for those who are strong to enter the kingdom of God. Why is that? Rich people have a tendency to put their faith in their wealth; strong people in their strength; smart people in their intellect; beautiful people in their appearance. It just happens that riches are the key point in the society of the day. We all have a tendency to trust in our strong points, and for this man, that strong point was wealth.

Jesus answers their question, "Who can be saved?" by saying, "With men it is impossible, but not with God; for all things are possible with God" (10:27). Look at what Peter says. "Lo, we have left everything and followed you" (10:28). In contemporary English, what is He really saying? "Look at all we've given up! Aren't we going to get anything out of it? Aren't we going to be rich, too?" This is the Lord's answer. "Peter, if you think that riches are a blessing from God, you're missing what blessings really mean." He says you're going to receive in abundance, and He also says it is going to come with persecution. But those things aren't the key. If all we're looking for is to be rich, or strong, or smart, or beautiful, then we're missing what the kingdom of God is all about.

Omnipotence—A Standard of Power

Remember His words. "With men it is impossible, but not with God; for all things are possible with God" (10:27). Do you see a little bit about the power of God? He has given to us two great standards of His power, omnipresence and omniscience, but often we miss that the reality of His power is what He is willing to do day by day in our lives. All His power is available to us. In the Old Testament, God chose a people who we call the people of Israel. Abraham was the first Israelite and through a series of events, the Israelites ended up down in Egypt as a slave people. The man, Moses, who was to be their deliverer, ended up a failure out in the desert. He tried and didn't succeed because he tried in his own might and in his own power, and he ran away across the desert for 40 years, keeping sheep. Can you imagine what it was like to go from the palace of Pharaoh to the home of a wandering desert sheepherder with a houseful of daughters? Guess who ended up taking care of the sheep? From there he got a vision from God that he would be the deliverer. He argued with God that it wasn't possible for him to carry out the task, but finally God sent him back to deliver his people and to deliver them in such a way that everyone would know that only God could have done it. No army, no swords, no display of power on the part of people was evident. Rather, everything that happened was a sign from God.

Moses is not only a leader and a great man of God, who is able to deliver his people, but he is also a poet.

> I will sing to the Lord, for he has triumphed gloriously;
> the horse and his rider he has thrown into the sea.
> The Lord is my strength and my song,
> and he has become my salvation;
> this is my God, and I will praise him,
> my father's God, and I will exalt him.
> The Lord is a man of war; the Lord is his name.
>
> Pharaoh's chariots and his host he cast into the sea;
> and his picked officers are sunk in the Red Sea.
> The floods cover them; they went down into the depths like a stone.

Thy right hand, O Lord, glorious in power,
  thy right hand, O Lord, shatters the enemy.
In the greatness of thy majesty thou overthrowest thy adversaries;
  thou sendest forth thy fury, it consumes them like stubble.
At the blast of thy nostrils the waters piled up,
  the floods stood up in a heap;
  the deeps congealed in the heart of the sea.

The enemy said, 'I will pursue, I will overtake,
  I will divide the spoil, my desire shall have its fill of them.
  I will draw my sword, my hand shall destroy them.'

Thou didst blow with thy wind, the sea covered them;
  they sank as lead in the mighty waters.
Who is like thee, O Lord, among the gods?
  Who is like thee, majestic in holiness,
  terrible in glorious deeds, doing wonders?
Thou didst stretch out thy right hand, the earth swallowed them

          (Exod. 15:1–12).

Time after time in the Old Testament, we see that the God of Israel is called the God who brought the people up out of Egypt. Do you see why? Theirs is a standard of power for what God can do, for what God will do, and for what God had done. Based upon this experience, God expected them to be able to go on, to worship Him, to follow Him, to conquer the land and be His people. Throughout the Old Testament this becomes the standard of God's power for His people.

We can see this standard of power manifested throughout the New Testament, as well. Time and again Paul teaches on this very subject. In Ephesians, Paul has told the people about God's great salvation for us, planned by the Father, accomplished by the Son, and applied to us by the Holy Spirit. Therefore, he says, "For this reason, because I have heard of your faith in the Lord Jesus and your love toward all the saints, I do not cease to give thinks for you, remembering you in my prayers, that the God of our Lord Jesus Christ, the Father of glory, may give you a spirit of wisdom and of revelation in the knowledge of him" (1:15–17). The key to his prayer is that we may be given a spirit of wisdom and revelation in knowing God.

In connection with God's power, let's consider some

thoughts brought forth in the New Testament. Once again we see the basis of this to be the standard of power in the Old Testament—the God who brought the Israelites up out of bondage in Egypt. The promise is that "the God who brought you up out of Egypt will take care of you." The New Testament standard of power is Jesus, ". . . that you may know what is the hope to which he has called you, what are the riches of his glorious inheritance in the saints, and what is the immeasurable greatness of his power in us who believe, according to the working of his great might which he accomplished in Christ when he raised him from the dead and made him sit at his right hand in the heavenly places, far above all rule and authority and power and dominion, and above every name that is named, not only in this age but also in that which is to come; and he has put all things under his feet and has made him the head over all things for the church, which is his body, the fulness of him who fills all in all" (Eph. 1:18–23). The climax of Paul's prayer is that we might know the power of God—power that raised Jesus from the dead. Can you think of any problems bigger than that one?

Take note of three things that Paul said. First of all, remember that we can claim a hope. Also remember what the riches are which are our inheritance, and take heed of the immeasurable greatness of God's power. What is the greatness of his power that can't be measured? It is that God took a man, Son of God, Son of man, raised Him from the dead and made Him the sovereign and the Lord of everything in this universe. Can you understand the extent of God's power? He conquered death, He conquered time and space, He conquered sin, and He displays His glory by placing His Son as Lord of all. This is the immeasurable greatness of His power.

Omnipotence—The Power of God in Us

The first few phrases of Psalm 139 are about the knowledge of God. He knows us so totally that He knows our thoughts even before we think them, and our words before we say them. Secondly, it is impossible to escape God's presence because wherever we go, He is there. And now He speaks of

God's creative power. "For thou didst form my inward parts, thou didst knit me together in my mother's womb. I praise thee, for thou art fearful and wonderful. Wonderful are thy works! Thou knowest me right well; my frame was not hidden from thee, when I was being made in secret, intricately wrought in the depths of the earth, Thy eyes beheld my unformed substance; in thy book were written, every one of them, the days that were formed for me, when as yet there was none of them" (Ps. 139:13–16).

If you have studied modern biology or genetics, you know that inside the female are hundreds of thousands of eggs, and hundreds of thousands of sperm are in the male. Modern scientists say that by chance a certain egg comes down the tube to be fertilized by a single sperm. Within the coding of the genes of that egg and that sperm is all that it takes to make a person—every part of us—skin, hair, eyes, coloring, the shape of our nose is all there, and according to some scientists, personality traits as well. All of this happens by chance, so say the scientists of the day; everyone of us is no more than a chance happening of the collision of egg and sperm with no one in control. What does the psalmist say in regard to how we are made? He says it poetically. He didn't understand modern science; he never had a course in genetics; he probably had no idea of how it happens that babies are formed from man and woman. He goes one step further, though, and says that we aren't born by chance. Rather he knows that God formed us. God chose the egg and the sperm and made us exactly the way we are.

Our inward parts, as the psalmist calls them, refer to our emotions. What we are as personality is woven together before we are born. We've gone through swings of the pendulum in psychological understanding from saying that everything we are is hereditary, to saying that everything is caused by the environment. Now we're swinging back toward the middle and establishing some percentages. It is clear in Scripture that God has designed a law by which you reap what you sow, and that's not just bad deeds, that is good deeds, too. We are shaped by the deeds that we do, by the home that we're in, by the company we keep, by what we do with our spare time. Therefore environmental shaping is very important and is clearly outlined in Scripture.

Something else is also clear, and that is genetic shaping. David is saying here that some of what we are—some of the emotional structure of what we are, is God-designed. I don't know if there is such a thing as a perfect temperament, but God has put us together uniquely. Therefore we are fearfully and wonderfully made.

The emotional side of life is often denied in a male-oriented world. Our society is one which does not cry and it does not laugh. Sometimes it can get excited only at a football game, it does not reveal hurt, and it can't lose its temper. Much of the structure of the expression of personality is taken away. But our emotions are real and they, too, are God-designed to be dealt with in that perspective. Many times in the Old Testament, God is spoken of as being angry. A healthy anger, if you will, is sometimes good, as long as in our anger we are careful not to sin or let the sun go down on our wrath. You see, we have been carefully knit together and the sum of our beings, our personalities, our thoughts and minds, our physical appearances were carefully and lovingly designed by a God who is all-powerful and still in control of who we are.

Although we may think differently, it is no mistake that some people are five feet, two inches, or that some people have curly hair, or crooked noses, or have to wear glasses. Somehow through all of the things which we consider unsightly in ourselves, the psalmist is saying that in the greatness of God's power, He designs what we are as a person. He designs what we are in our physical stature and it's all within His purpose. It is very, very important that we hold to this belief.

Probably the most common emotion among teen-agers today is that they think nobody feels as they do. Nobody understands the way they think or act. Nobody else worries about their femininity, masculinity, sexuality, popularity, or any of the other fears that enter young minds. A healthy adult learns to accept what he is during those years. But we live in a terribly destructive world that says, "It is bad to be short or too tall or too thin or have too many freckles," or to have any of the slightest imperfections that make us what we are. We fight our God-given natures so hard! The psalmist is saying that God in his power designed us exactly the way He wanted us. We can distort that design either with our physical appearance or with our personalities. We don't need to try to rearrange the way that God made us, but we do need to let Him work within us.

Going one step further, we can know that each one of our days is designed for us, too. "Thy eyes beheld my unformed substance; in thy book were written, every one of them, the days that were formed for me, when as yet there was none of them" (139:16). God has designed not just who we are, not just what we are; but also He has designed the world in which we live, and He has made us for it. Unless we believe this, it can be hard sometimes to face the day. Our confidence can be in the truth that the days which we dread have already been laid out for us in the volume of God's Book, so that nothing will take place that is more than we can handle, that will be destructive to us, or that will hurt us in any way.

Recently I received a letter from a girl who at one time had been asked to leave school. Her conduct had become self-destructive and eventually she spent a couple of years in the counter culture. In her letter she explained about her present work with people who are just like she had been. Her comment was that those years when she had removed herself from the mainstream of society had been horrible; but they had prepared her for the work she is doing today. At one time I thought that the things happening to her were the worst things that could possibly happen to a girl and I wouldn't want her to go through it again, but God used it so that today she's thankful.

"We know that in everything God works for good with those who love him, who are called according to his purpose" (Rom. 8:28). Think also upon the verse, "No temptation has overtaken you that is not common to man. God is faithful, and he will not let you be tempted beyond your strength, but with the temptation will also provide the way of escape, that you may be able to endure it" (1 Cor. 10:13). These two verses contain what the psalmist was saying, that God has ordered our days and is at work. Therefore we can relax about them. If we know that nothing will happen in any given day beyond that which we are able to bear, then we will be amazed at what happens to our fears.

"How precious to me are thy thoughts, O God! How vast is the sum of them! If I would count them, they are more than the sand. When I awake, I am still with thee" (Ps. 139:17–18). "Search me, O God, and know my heart! Try me and know my thoughts! And see if there be any wicked way in me, and lead me in the way everlasting!" (139:23–24). Do you see the sequence? God is all-knowing. "Thou art acquainted with all my ways" (139:3). God is all-present. "Where shall I go from thy Spirit?" (139:7). God is all-powerful. "The days that were formed for me, when as yet there was none of them" (139:16). Ordering one's life seems like a simple thing. But think of the thousands of years of history and the billions of people, and consider what God does to order all of our lives. His promise is that He will never forsake us, and also that not one of His people will stand before Him and accuse Him of being unfair and unjust.

Omnipotence—God Is Able

God's power is seen from another perspective in Matthew 3. John the Baptist is out preaching in the wilderness. "But when he saw many of the Pharisees and Sadducees coming for baptism, he said to them, 'You brood of vipers! Who warned you to flee from the wrath to come? Bear fruit that befits repentance, and do not presume to say to yourselves, "We have Abraham as our father"; for I tell you, God is able from these stones to raise up children to Abraham'" (3:7–9). What is happening to the Jewish people? Perhaps they are suffering from too much pride and a little bit of confidence in who their father is. What is God able to do with them? He is able to make people out of stones if He wants to. In His grace, God

114

uses us, but He really doesn't need us. We aren't so crucial to His plan that He cannot use someone else just as well. If He can make people from stones, just think what He could do with us if we'd only let Him!

In the Book of Jude it is written in the benediction, "Now to him who is able to keep you from falling and to present you without blemish before the presence of his glory with rejoicing, to the only God, our Savior through Jesus Christ our Lord, be glory, majesty, dominion, and authority, before all time and now and forever" (24–25). God's hand is upon us and He is able to keep us from falling. He doesn't say that we will not stumble, but when we do, He is there to keep it from being a headlong fall. The second step is that after He is done, He can present us without any scars. That is one of the most beautiful promises of Scripture. When we are before Him, all blemishes will be gone.

Further, Paul has written, "Now to him who by the power at work within us is able to do far more abundantly than all that we ask or think, to him be glory in the church and in Christ Jesus to all generations, for ever and ever" (Eph. 3:20–21). What is God able to do? He can accomplish more than we can even think or ask. I'm convinced that more of our prayers get answered than we think. It is just that we miss the answers because we're expecting so little. Remember the prayer meeting in Acts 12. Peter is in jail, James is dead, and they're all gathered praying about Peter and whoever might be next? Is it any wonder that the disciples prayed fervently? But when the knock came on the door and the little girl heard Peter's voice, what did she do? She was so shocked that God had answered their prayer that she didn't let him in. When she went into the prayer meeting to tell them that Peter was there, they wouldn't believe her. Can you hear them tell her to be quiet because they were praying? The exciting perspective which we can grasp is that the power of God is not limited, especially not limited by our expectations. He is able to do exceeding abundantly in our lives and He always does what is the best for us.

STUDY QUESTIONS

1. How does Paul describe God's power in Ephesians 3:20–21? How did Paul learn about this in his lifetime? (See Acts 9, Acts 16:26, Acts 20:9–12.)

2. In Acts 12 when Peter was in jail, there is a good illustration of God doing more than anybody thought He could. What happened? What did the people pray? Did they believe God would answer? Why did God answer their prayer?

3. In Jude 24, the Bible says, "Now unto Him who is able to keep you from falling and to present you without blemish before the presence of His glory . . . " What is God able to do for us?

4. In Ephesians 1:19–20, Paul tells us about God's most powerful act. What is it? What does it mean to us?

12

God Is Sovereign

Illustrations of the Sovereignty of God

Our consideration of the sovereignty of God begins with Abraham, the father of the nation of Israel; Isaac, the son of promise; and Jacob, the younger of twins. God's choice, Jacob, feels he has to scheme a little bit in order to get his birthright, so he and his mother scheme against Esau and his father. Jacob gets the birthright and runs away from home. He comes back, having been married to Leah under false pretenses, and then to Rachel. Several years later, he has picked up two more wives and has fathered twelve sons. This is the history of the family of Jacob. "Joseph, being seventeen years old, was shepherding the flock with his brothers; he was a lad with the sons of Bilhah and Zilpah, his father's wives; and Joseph brought an ill report of them to their father" (Gen. 37:2). Can you tell what kind of a household Jacob lives in? It is a house with multiple wives, tattletale children, a divided family, and abounding favoritism. Joseph was favored by his father and he was the one to receive the special multi-colored robe. His brothers, however, "saw that their father loved him more than all his brothers, they hated him, and could not speak peaceably to him" (37:4).

"Now Joseph had a dream, and when he told it to his brothers they only hated him the more. He said to them,

'Hear this dream which I have dreamed: behold we were binding sheaves in the field, and lo, my sheaf arose and stood upright; and behold, your sheaves gathered around it, and bowed down to my sheaf'" (37:5–7). Does this make you love Joseph any more? "His brothers said to him, 'Are you indeed to reign over us? Or are you indeed to have dominion over us?' So they hated him yet more for his dreams and for his words. Then he dreamed another dream, and told it to his brothers, and said, 'Behold, I have dreamed another dream; and behold, the sun, the moon, and eleven stars were bowing down to me'" (37:8–9). Would you love Joseph? Not only were his brothers jealous, but he provoked their jealousy. Isn't it fascinating how he told the dream? He couldn't resist counting the stars and telling his brothers.

"But when he told it to his father and to his brothers, his father rebuked him, and said to him, 'What is this dream that you have dreamed? Shall I and your mother and your brothers indeed come to bow ourselves to the ground before you?' And his brothers were jealous of him, but his father kept the saying in mind" (37:10–11). Do you suppose the father was thinking that Joseph shouldn't have told his brothers, but since he already had, he shouldn't stop in the middle of the stream? You see, his father is hearing, and probably liking, what he hears. This is his favorite son who is a little bit spunky, a little bit of a dreamer. So it is all right if he can get somewhere. And Daddy loves him for it even though he reacts against the way his son is handling his dreams.

As the story progresses, Joseph was sent to deliver some food to his brothers who were pasturing the flocks. "They saw him afar off, and before he came near to them they conspired against him to kill him. They said one to another, 'Here comes this dreamer. Come now, let us kill him and throw him into one of the pits; then we shall say that a wild beast has devoured him, and we shall see what will become of his dreams.' But when Reuben heard it, he delivered him out of their hands, saying, 'Let us not take his life.' And Reuben said to them, 'Shed no blood; cast him into this pit here in the wilderness, but lay no hand upon him'—that he might rescue him out of their hand, to restore him to his father" (37:18–22).

Imagine what it would be like if you were Joseph. You are a slave, following somebody's camel into Egypt. What are you thinking? *Will I ever get back?* Perhaps even more ominous would be thoughts of your brothers. Had Joseph not mentioned his dreams at all, things would have been different. Here the story divides, and I want you to think about it in two ways. The older brothers take the coat home to their father, saying that his son must have been killed, because they found his coat.

"And he recognized it, and said, 'It is my son's robe; a wild beast has devoured him; Joseph is without doubt torn to pieces.' Then Jacob rent his garments, and put sackcloth upon his loins, and mourned for his son many days. All his sons and all his daughters rose up to comfort him; but he refused to be comforted, and said, 'No I shall go down to Sheol to my son, mourning.' Thus his father wept for him" (37:33–35).

Put yourself in the place of one of the sons. What are you telling your dad? Maybe it is the usual funeral remarks you're saying: "Oh, he's better off where he is now than if he were here," or something similar. But deep inside, what are you thinking? Did it change the home to get rid of Joseph? Imagine what it would be like. Joseph ends up staying down in Egypt for a minimum of eleven or twelve years before he rejoins his family. So for at least twelve years, they are living that lie to their father. If they had really wanted to, they could have gone to find Joseph. On one hand, they are comforting their father, and on the other hand, they refuse to do anything about it. It is hard to believe they hated Joseph so much and would do nothing about their father's grief.

While in Egypt, Joseph became very successful. "Now Joseph was taken down to Egypt, and Potiphar, an officer of Pharaoh, the captain of the guard, an Egyptian, bought him from the Ishmaelites who had brought him down there" (39:1). During his stay, Potiphar's wife tried to seduce him and he ended up in jail falsely accused. Interestingly enough, he had taken a stand for right. "But he refused [to lie with her] and said to his master's wife, 'Lo, having me my master has no concern about anything in the house, and he has put everything that he has in my hand; he is not greater in this house than am I; nor has he kept back anything from me except yourself, because you are his wife; how then can I do this great wickedness, and sin against God?' " (39:8–9). How do you perceive Joseph? What could he have done? When someone has acted wrongly against you, do you ever get tempted to say, "Well, Lord, now that You've forgotten me, I can do whatever I want." All of Joseph's dreams are dead. There is no room for them in Egypt from any human perspective. Yet he still stands on his integrity. Even though he wasn't a very nice brother, on the other hand, he's a pretty remarkable man because he stands up for something and stays with it.

After a brief time, a couple of officers end up in jail with him. Joseph sees a way out and says he will tell them their dreams if they won't forget him and possibly return the favor someday. It seems as if things will work out favorably, except "the chief butler did not remember Joseph, but forgot him" (40:23). What happens after two whole years when you've been sold into slavery, betrayed into jail, and have tried without success to get out? How do you think Joseph felt about what happened to him?

Two Perspectives on the Sovereignty of God

With that as a background, the Psalms can further enlighten our thinking about the sovereignty of God. Psalm 105 is a psalm of the goodness of God and of praise to the Lord for his faithfulness to His covenant. "When they were few in number, of little account, and sojourners in it, wandering from nation to nation, from one kingdom to another people, he allowed no one to oppress them; he rebuked kings on their account, saying, 'Touch not my anointed ones, do my prophets no harm!' " (105:12–15). Abraham and his family are wandering around the land of promise, not possessing it, and facing an easy possibility of being wiped out except that God is taking care of them.

"When he summoned a famine on the land, and broke every staff of bread, he had sent a man ahead of them, Joseph, who was sold as a slave" (105:16–17). God caused the famine by taking away the bread. Do you believe that He is in charge of famines and rainstorms and cloudy days? If He isn't, then nobody is. But notice that He not only sent the famine, but also a way of dealing with it, because He already had Joseph in Egypt, a slave and in jail. "His feet were hurt with fetters, his neck was put in a collar of iron; until what he had said came to pass the word of the Lord tested him" (105:18–19). What does it take for a boy to go from about thirteen or fourteen to twenty-one years of age? That growing up process requires a lot of patience on the part of the parents, but from the boy is required a few dreams, some pressures, disappointments, and some struggling. Most of us don't make it by the time we reach twenty-one. In fact, growth during those years between eighteen and twenty-one is sort of fictitious, because some of us are still growing up when we reach forty. Was Joseph getting prepared to be a ruler by living with Jacob? What did it take to get him ready? It took some rough years, a lot of standing by principle, and it took a lot of obedience, because in seven years of plenty, what is the temptation? Wouldn't it be tempting to forget God and enjoy it? You see, for seven years, Joseph continued to be faithful to that dream of plenty and the wealth and honor which accompany it.

Two perspectives are interrelated here. One is the human perspective, full of the failure, the joys, the freedom, the hurt. Even while the brothers were threatening to kill Joseph, God was doing what needed to be done in Joseph's life. This is such a fabulous story, because ultimately Joseph ends up with the next favored son, Benjamin, and the brothers have to go back and report one more time that another son is lost. Do you think the older brothers learned something out of all this? It took some years of guilt, some years of famine, the horror of living with a lie to teach them. Who knows who else God was working with at the same time? "We know that in everything God works for good with those who love him, who are called according to his purpose" (Rom. 8:28). Do you believe that even when things do not go well that God is still working in your life? We all struggle because we don't see the beginning or even the end as well as we would like. As a result, we get caught in the middle. And Paul says that "we know that in everything, God is at work for good to those who love him, to those who are called according to his purpose."

That's a fascinating bunch of words, isn't it? We *know* this, yet we struggle with that knowledge quite a lot. We love God, not as perfectly as we ought or we might, but we do love him. We know that in everything—rainstorms, famines, sales contracts, imprisonments, dreams—in *everything*, God is at work. One of the greatest things we can learn to say is that God is working. God is at work *for* good. Notice that it doesn't say that God is making everything happen, neither does it say that everything that happens is good. This is why the Psalm starts out, "O give thanks to the Lord, call on his name, make known his deeds among the peoples! Sing to him, sing praises to him, tell of all his wonderful works! Glory in his holy name; let the hearts of those who seek the Lord rejoice! Seek the Lord and his strength, seek his presence continually! Remember the wonderful works that he has done, his miracles, and the judgments he uttered, O offspring of Abraham his servant, sons of Jacob, his chosen ones!" (105:1–6).

Mankind has a greater ability to remember what went wrong, to remember the disappointments, the unfavorable incidences, and the unanswered prayers. One day I was really jolted when I sat down to make a list of answered prayers and unanswered prayers. The unanswered list seemed the longest, but as I thought about it, sometimes those prayers which appeared unanswered were prayers that God had answered in His own way and in His own time. But, you see, the Psalm is telling us to give thanks to the Lord, to call upon Him, to remember His wonderful works. One of the proofs of this direction for our lives is Joseph.

The Extent of God's Sovereignty

Centuries later, God brought the Israelites into the land, and gave them their kings. Finally he had to take the northern kings in judgment and then send Nebuchadnezzar to take Judah, Benjamin, and the last tribes captive. In the custom of

Oriental emperors, they went in, conquered them, and took out the best leadership. They took out enough of the people to demoralize the populace and to destroy the power of the nation to resist. In taking out the leadership, they took out four young men. Daniel was of the tribe of Judah, the kingly line. One of the most princely men that Israel ever had was left without a choice of what he could do. Unlike some men in America during the sixties who resisted conflict, he couldn't become a conscientious objector, he couldn't flee to Canada. He had to become submissive to the nation and its government. "But Daniel resolved that he would not defile himself" (Dan. 1:8).

His first test was what he could eat. My temptation would have been to at least try what was available to eat. But Daniel didn't, and God honored that discipline and gave him an opportunity to reveal Nebuchadnezzar's dream, a dream about an image with a golden head, silver breastplate, bronze lower parts, and iron legs, which was destroyed. And Daniel told Nebuchadnezzar that there would be four great world empires before God would destroy them and establish His own. When Daniel was finished, Nebuchadnezzar honored him for interpreting his dream, because it had seemed to the king an impossible task. Perhaps for a while, Nebuchadnezzar remembered about the God of the dream, but then he forgot and thought about the head of gold instead.

Nebuchadnezzar built an image ninety feet high and eight feet wide, then called all the leadership of the nation to him and commanded them to bow down. But three people didn't bow down, and those three people were the ones who were captured at the same time Daniel had been taken captive. When the king confronted them, and said that anyone not bowing to his image would be cast into a fiery furnace, they replied, "O Nebuchadnezzar, we have no need to answer you in this matter. If it be so, our God whom we serve is able to deliver us from the burning fiery furnace; and he will deliver us out of your hand, O king. But if not, be it known to you, O king, that we will not serve your gods or worship the golden image which you have set up" (3:16–18). Note that they say their God is able to deliver them and that He will deliver them.

Nebuchadnezzar was furious and in his wrath caused the deaths of a group of his own men as they tried to throw Meshach, Shadrach, and Abednego into the fire. "Then King Nebuchadnezzar was astonished and rose up in haste. He said to his counselors, 'Did we not cast three men bound into the fire?' They answered the king, 'True, O king.' He answered, 'But I see four men loose, walking in the midst of the fire, and they are not hurt; and the appearance of the fourth is like a son of the gods' " (3:24–25). The emperor learned more about God—particularly that God's power was greater than his own.

Then Nebuchadnezzar dreamed another dream about a great tree that ultimately was cut down. For seven years it rotted and was ruined, and then it was raised up. He asked Daniel to interpret that dream. Daniel said that the tree was Nebuchadnezzar and he would be out of the kingdom for seven years in order to learn who God really is. The king heard the interpretation, but once again forgot it. But, "All this came upon King Nebuchadnezzar. At the end of twelve months he was walking on the roof of the royal palace of Babylon, and the king said, "Is not this great Babylon, which I have built by my mighty power as a royal residence and for the glory of my majesty?" (4:28–30). Had he forgotten that he ruled only because God had given him the kingdom, and then only by God's power? He had slipped and said, "Look what *I* have done."

"While the words were still in the king's mouth, there fell a voice from heaven, 'O King Nebuchadnezzar, to you it is spoken: The kingdom has departed from you, and you shall be driven from among men, and your dwelling shall be with the beasts of the field; and you shall be made to eat grass like an ox; and seven times shall pass over you, until you have learned that the Most High rules the kingdom of men and gives it to whom he will.' Immediately the word was fulfilled upon Nebuchadnezzar. He was driven from among men, and ate grass like an ox, and his body was wet with the dew of heaven till his hair grew as long as eagles' feathers, and his nails were like birds' claws" (4:31–33). The greatest emperor of his period in history became incompetent to rule over his kingdom.

"At the end of the days I, Nebuchadnezzar, lifted my eyes to heaven, and my reason returned to me, and I blessed the Most High, and praised and honored him who lives forever; for his dominion is an everlasting dominion, and his kingdom endures from generation to generation; all the inhabitants of the earth are accounted as nothing; and he does according to his will in the host of heaven and among the inhabitants of the earth; and none can stay his hand or say to him, 'What doest thou?' " (4:34–35). This is a clear example of how God gives man a freedom, an opportunity to do and to choose; but God is also at work, one time in a prison, the next time in a palace in Babylon. Neither Joseph nor Nebuchadnezzar escaped the working of God and the realization that God is good, that He is sovereign, that He is in control of His world.

Do you see that no one escapes God's working? Sometime, somewhere in life, everyone comes face to face with that reality. It is at such a time that we are made supremely aware of the sovereignty of God and His claim upon our lives.

STUDY QUESTIONS

1. Is the world we live in an ordered, structured world, or is it chaotic and random?

2. Often we quote Romans 8:28 in times of tragedy or hardship. What are we inferring about God's power and control when we do this?

3. What is the role of the sovereignty of God and the security of salvation? (Romans 8:31–39.)

4. What is the role of failure in this world? (John 9:3, 11:14 and 15; Luke 22, 23, 31, and 32.)

13

"That I May Know Him"

Understanding the attributes of God is a task worthy of our most diligent study. As we remain open to being led by the Spirit of God, His characteristics will become more and more a part of our daily lives.

There are several study and prayer groups which meet each week in our town and God has used those times very specially as a time to make His characteristics known. One gentleman in particular is a spectacular example of God working in our lives. For many years, he was an outstanding surgeon, well known and highly respected in his chosen field of medicine. Ten years ago this man contracted Parkinson's disease and today he uses a medication made available to only 300 people world wide.

We have shared many conversations in the days we have spent together and once I asked him what had been the hardest thing to accept about being forced out of a promising career because of his illness. He thought a long time and finally was able to express that he could no longer do anything well. To sit across from a man who had been the leading surgeon in his town before he became ill and to realize that the years of training and practice culminated in his not being able to do anything well professionally was a striking experience. You see, rather than change this man's body, God chose to reveal himself by transforming my friend's heart.

God brings lessons home for us to learn sometimes. Several weeks later I spent some time hospitalized for an appendectomy. As I laid in the hospital, not knowing at first what was wrong, I turned to Scripture asking God for some kind of message. I found in Jeremiah a very helpful thought for the time, "They will fight against you; but they shall not prevail against you, for I am with you, says the Lord, to deliver you" (1:19). I asked the Lord that as long as I remained there the room would be a place where He lived, a place where His presence would be known. Those days in the hospital were miserable days, but in the midst of the pain was the reality of the presence of God. I continued reading in Jeremiah about God's complaint against Israel. "The priests did not say, 'Where is the Lord?' Those who handle the law did not know me" (2:8). What a tragic commentary on the leadership of a nation—the spiritual leadership of a nation! Those who were in responsible positions to carry out the law did not know God. With great consistency the thoughts from God came to mind, "Why are you worrying? We're together." Out of these moments, again came the question, "They knew the Law. Do you know the Law? They didn't know God. Do you know God?"

There is a great danger in learning theology and studying the Bible, but still not knowing God. This is entirely possible. In fact, it happens far too often and some of the foremost commentaries around today are written by men who don't know God; men who have helped with insight into grammar, words, references, and history—but they do not know God. The opposite of this, then, is the encouragement to study the Scriptures with these tools so that we may come to an understanding of who God is—the God who art in heaven.

Think with me about Paul's statement in Philippians 3, "That I may know Him" (3:10). Notice that this is not a lengthy list of goals to accomplish within a few months or a year, as so many of us who are familiar with modern management principles try to attain. There is an old story about a fellow who noticed several bull's eyes on the side of a barn with holes in the middle. When he inquired about such excellent marksmanship, the fellow said that he shot first and then drew the bull's eyes. If life is going to fit together at all, the overriding target in our lives which should be our constant goal, is to know God. That is the only way we can know life and understand how it works—"That I may know Him and the power of His resurrection."

Knowing God in His Power

In Christ's life we see the tremendous impact of His power to heal. In John 5, for example, we see the lame man who was sitting near the pool and was asked if he wanted to be healed. I think he was probably one of the first sign carriers. He sat on the edge of the crowd rather than the edge of the pool proclaiming that he had been there longer than anybody else, as he began rattling his cup. He didn't really want to be healed because it was more enjoyable to blame someone else for his infirmities. The Lord ruined his collection agency by healing the man who for 38 years had not figured out how to get closer to the water. As he carried his bed through the temple area he was questioned about doing that on the Sabbath day. He responded that it was Jesus' fault because He had told him to carry his bed. We see him in a transformed body, but an unchanged person. He had seen the power of God in his body, but he hadn't known the power that changes lives—and that is the power of the Resurrection. That is why the Lord says to His disciples that they would do greater things than He had done. Ours is a ministry of Resurrection life, a ministry of a poured-out Holy Spirit that transforms people.

The question then becomes: Are we knowing today that power which transforms our lives? One way to know someone is to find out what he does and what he can do. But do we do that? Having been reared in a fundamentalist home where the measurement is against perfection, having been for most of my adult life involved with education and having taught for about 15 years, I gained a strong ability to look at a paper and determine what was wrong with it, or to look at people and decide what was wrong with them. In the years since I have been crucially aware of an ability to see things negatively, I've asked the Lord to change forty years of measuring against perfection. I've asked to be a Barnabas, an encourager, to be one who sees how people have grown, not how they fall short. I want to see what God is doing in peoples' lives, rather than see what I wish He would do. Many people are put down because they are not yet perfect, rather than encouraged and built up for their potential to become what God would have them to be. The power of God changes how we think, how we respond to people. We see the lake not through the eyes of a fisherman who says daytime is the wrong time to fish, but through the eyes of the Creator, who sees fish waiting to be caught. This is the power of God's resurrection—the fellowship of His suffering.

Knowing God Through His Emotions

We can become closer to knowing God because we can see in Scripture how He feels. Most of us have learned to mask how we feel. We can read Zane Grey and learn how the gunfighters never flinched before they drew a pistol, shot, and accomplished the purpose of their day. Many of us have modeled our own lives after the western hero by pulling the mask over our faces so that no one really knows the feelings behind the facades. Not only does the mask prevent knowledge of how we feel, but also of who we are. The opposite of this then is Paul's statement: "That I may know him, the fellowship, that I may share in His suffering."

In John 11, we can see the miracle of Lazarus and begin to understand how the Lord shows us His feelings. Look at those verses under the heading, "Jesus loved Martha, Mary, and Lazarus" (11:5). Here is a chapter on loving three people. We come down to that short verse so many of us memorized early because it consists of only two words, "Jesus wept" (11:35). Try to look at that verse through the eyes of love. It would have been easy to see it the way most men handle crying women—to ask them to stop crying and to tell them that everything will work out and be O.K. Can you see yourself saying that to Mary? The reality of Jesus' response to Mary's tears is that He wept with her, in spite of the fact that He knew the outcome. He shared in the struggle, in the suffering, in the groaning of the crowds, yet knowing the results of those days. But He openly shared in His feelings with those who were there. Have you begun to have a heart for people? Have you cried with anyone lately? Or laughed?

Sometimes we don't really think we should share our feelings at all, even though we know that such a holding back of who we are keeps us from being known. I have a friend who for several years has told me that one of his ministries is the joy of laughter, of bringing to people the relaxation of laughing together. I have watched day after day his ability of bringing joy and laughter to people. You see, God laughs. I don't think you can read Scripture people-wise without seeing some of the humor in many chapters, because of the irony that is so often there. Yet crying is in many of those same chapters because God doesn't sit up in the heavens reading the morning paper rejoicing in our suffering. We ask how a good and loving God can have an evil world like this, as if we're the ones who would do it differently, when a good and loving God suffers and consistently loves in a world like this.

Knowing God in Death

The result of knowing someone is becoming like him in the greatest things that he does. Read this verse in Philippians once again: "That I may know the power of His resurrection, and may share His sufferings, becoming like Him in His death" (3:10). Is the greatest thing which God has done for us having any effect on our lives? Are we becoming like Him in His death? Do we understand what He did? Do we live that way?

It has been said that a couple often begins to look alike after they have been married for some years. Paul's third step in knowing God is becoming like Him in God's greatest act of love toward us—the death of His Son. That is the lifestyle of Christianity—the mind of Christ. That we pour our life into others just as He poured His life into humanity and became obedient unto death—the death of the cross. For us this death is not just the way we will die some day. But it is the pattern of life that we die to ourselves, our self-gratification, our possessions, our desires. We are no longer living under the control of the flesh, but we are living under Christ's control.

Knowing God produces a subtle change in the way we think. It changes how we see theology and Greek and the Bible and history and Christian education and relationships. It changes the Bible from a textbook into a living Book that is telling us all about a person. It changes how we pray. Often our prayers become so routine, so predictable, so automatic. Then we realize that we aren't really talking to God so much as we are reminding Him to do something about this or that, as if He hadn't heard it before and didn't know. It changes the way we see people—we begin to see them in the way God sees them. It changes the way we see our families. It changes how we see ourselves. Have you ever felt as if you were a person in tow, on the way somewhere, not functioning very well, but nevertheless, on the way? In our performance-oriented "doing world" it is easy to call that lifestyle Christian and say we're doing that for God. My friend for whom this is impossible because of his disease is learning a higher goal in life—and that is knowing God and becoming like Him regardless of his ability to perform. You see, as our desire increasingly becomes to know God and to share in His fellowship, then we will experience the joy of a transformed heart, of a heart that with greater consistency seeks to discover the attributes of God.

> Father, our desire is to know you. Our longing is to do that, but it is so easy to get crowded in time and thought by the busyness of all that surrounds us and would control us. Change us, Father, we who do our work because it is there to be done, have devotions simply because it is that time of day, witness or share because that is part of our job. Change us from routine living to people who know you and in whose lives You are reflected.